I0605978

DISEASES WITHOUT BORDERS

Plagues, Pandemics, and Beyond

Marc Zimmer

TWENTY-FIRST CENTURY BOOKS / MINNEAPOLIS

For my mother

Twenty-First Century Books™
An imprint of Lerner Publishing Group, Inc.
241 First Avenue North
Minneapolis, MN 55401 USA

For reading levels and more information, look up this title at www.lernerbooks.com.

Diagram on p. 77 by Laura K. Westlund.
Main body text set in Adobe Garamond Pro.
Typeface provided by Adobe Systems.

Library of Congress Cataloging-in-Publication Data

Names: Zimmer, Marc author
Title: Diseases without borders : plagues, pandemics, and beyond / Marc Zimmer.
Description: Minneapolis, MN : Twenty-First Century Books, 2026. | Includes bibliographical references and index. | Audience: Ages 11–18 | Audience: Grades 7–9 | Summary: “Dive into how major diseases work, how they spread, where they are now, and more in this thorough overview”— Provided by publisher.
Identifiers: LCCN 2025017473 (print) | LCCN 2025017474 (ebook) | ISBN 9798765648070 library binding | ISBN 9798348000264 epub
Subjects: LCSH: Diseases—Juvenile literature | Diseases
Classification: LCC R130.5 .Z56 2026 (print) | LCC R130.5 (ebook) | DDC 616—dc23/eng/20250918

LC record available at https://lccn.loc.gov/2025017473
LC ebook record available at https://lccn.loc.gov/2025017474

Manufactured in the United States of America
1-1012838-53369-10/9/2025

CONTENTS

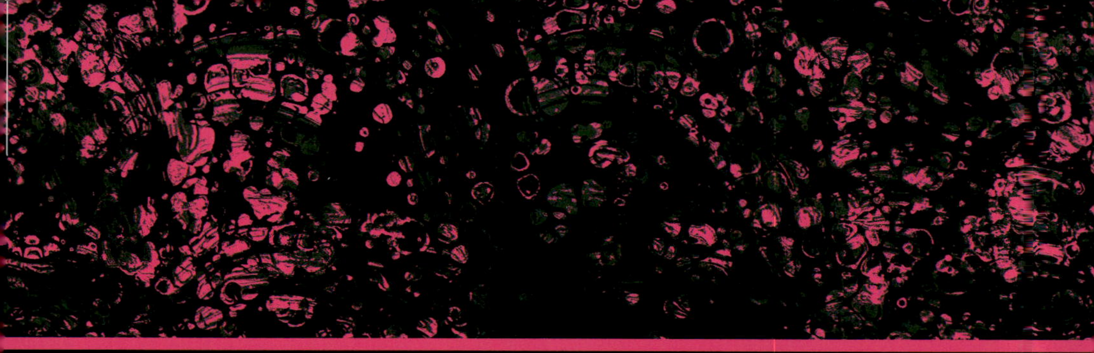

CHAPTER 1

THE PLAGUE AND PRE-INDUSTRIALIZATION PANDEMICS

The bubonic plague is often considered the greatest natural disaster in human history. From 1346 to 1666 BCE, it killed between eighty and two hundred million people across several outbreaks. This plague pandemic was also known as the Black Death, the Pestilence, and the Great Mortality. Its victims spat out blood, stank due to their rotting flesh, convulsively coughed, and had swellings called buboes.

Although it was the worst and most deadly outbreak of the plague, the Black Death was not the first or the last outbreak of the plague. Earlier outbreaks, such as the Plague of Justinian (about 541–542 BCE), had preceded the Black Death and its devastating consequences. The Plague of Justinian was named after the Byzantine Emperor Justinian I, who was a victim of the disease but survived it, unlike many others. Historians have estimated that the Plague of Justinian killed at least twenty-five million people in the Eastern Roman Empire (modern-day Italy, Greece, the Balkans, various Eastern Mediterranean countries, and North Africa), and some think it may have hastened the fall of the Roman Empire. The extensive loss of life also led to severe labor shortages and economic collapse after the Roman era.

CAUSES OF THE PLAGUE

During the Middle Ages (500–1500 CE), the cause of the Black Death was unknown, and people held various beliefs regarding the plague's origins. Many people believed the Black Death was a manifestation of the wrath of God, punishing humans for their sins and moral corruption. This belief was widespread and reinforced by religious authorities throughout the Middle Ages. Some sects, such as the flagellants (members of a Christian group who practiced self-whipping), took to public displays of penance, whipping themselves to atone for humanity's sins in hopes of ending the Black Death.

A medical theory centered on miasma, or "bad air," was also popular at the time. It proposed that "bad air" emanating from rotting organic matter caused diseases, including the plague and cholera. The theory was popular from the fourth century BCE to the 1880s CE, when the germ theory of diseases replaced it.

Germ theory is still the accepted theory for describing many diseases' origins. According to the theory, microorganisms known as germs, or pathogens, cause infectious diseases. There are many disease-causing pathogens, such as bacteria, viruses, fungi, parasites, and prions. When these organisms grow and reproduce, they cause diseases in their hosts. The germs are so tiny that they can only be seen under a microscope. Some, such as viruses and prions, are so small they can't even be seen under a light microscope.

The germ theory of diseases was a game changer in understanding the plague's origins. In 1894 a new wave of the plague hit Hong Kong, China. Within days of each other, two independent investigators, Alexandre Yersin and Shibasaburō Kitasato, discovered a new bacterium in Hong Kong plague patients. Kitasato found the bacteria a few days before Yersin, but Yersin received most of the credit because he could prove that the bacteria caused the plague. Yersin drained the buboes of deceased plague victims and identified the bacillus, a type of bacteria, under a microscope. Then he confirmed the involvement of the bacteria in plague infection by injecting healthy rodents with lymph

BACTERIA

Bacteria are single cellular life-forms. They can only be seen under a microscope and are present in virtually every environment on Earth, from soils and rocks to the ocean's depths, in the frigid polar snow, and inside all living organisms.

Earth formed around 4.6 billion years ago. According to fossil records, bacterial life emerged about a billion years later. The first *Homo sapiens*, or human, fossils only appeared around three hundred thousand years ago. If we scaled down the 4.6 billion years of Earth's existence into a single year, bacteria would have appeared in the early spring, with humans entering the scene a minuscule thirty minutes before midnight on December 31. Bacteria have been around for a long time.

Despite their tiny size, bacteria's collective biomass on Earth is tremendous, exceeding all animal mass by thirty-five times and human mass by a thousand. The human body has more bacteria than human cells. Most of these bacteria coexist with us as benign or even beneficial, especially in our digestive system, where they play essential roles in digestion and, strangely enough, in regulating our mental health. Only a small minority of bacteria in our bodies cause diseases by invading and damaging our tissues or by producing and releasing toxins that make us sick.

SHAPES OF BACTERIA

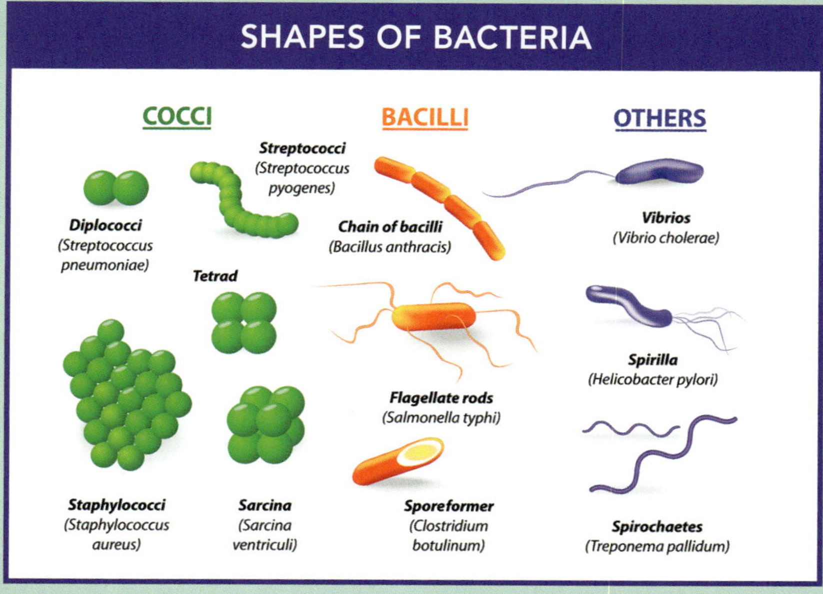

fluid extracted from infected mice. The healthy animals developed plague symptoms. Dissecting them showed that their blood and organs were filled with the plague bacillus. The bacterium responsible for the plague is called *Yersinia pestis* (*Y. pestis*).

Yersin and Kitasato figured out that bacteria caused the plague. But they hadn't proved who or what carried the bacteria. In 1898 French physician Paul-Louis Simond noticed that plague-infected rats that had recently died were more dangerous to handle because they were more likely to infect people, while infected rats that had been dead for several hours posed no risk. This suggested the existence of an external carrier of the plague bacteria that had left the dead rats. Simond also saw strange, unusually small "lesions" on infected people that looked like insect bites, leading him to suspect fleas were the carriers. To prove it, he caught fleas from a plague-infected rat and used them to infect a healthy rat, showing that fleas were spreading the disease. Initially, most of the scientific community didn't accept his findings, as insect-borne diseases were just being discovered. Other scientists later validated his conclusions, and by 1907 the community accepted them as scientific fact.

The scientific community soon understood the bubonic plague's whole pathogenesis (origin and development). The bubonic plague's primary transmission route is through the bite of an infected flea. When a healthy flea bites a bacterium-infected rodent, *Y. pestis* enters the flea's digestive system, forming a blockage in the midgut. In a flea that has not been infected, the blood meal from a bite passes straight into the stomach, satisfying the flea's appetite. But in a flea carrying the plague, the blockage deprives it of nourishment. It is perpetually hungry and constantly bites its hosts. The blood can't get past the blockage, building up in the flea's foregut, where it remains undigested. With each bite, the flea regurgitates infected blood, which contains the plague bacteria from prior bites, into the wound and the lymphatic system of the new host, thereby transmitting the disease. This cycle turns fleas into efficient vectors for spreading the plague among mammals. Humans aren't the

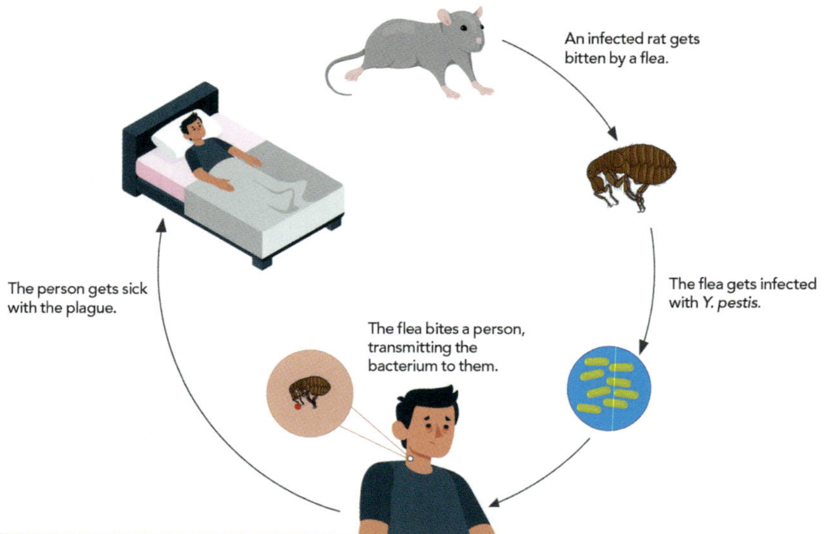

People are more likely to catch the plague in areas with higher populations of rats, such as big cities.

only victims. Cats, dogs, rabbits, camels, goats, and deer can also get the plague.

Thirty varied species of fleas both carry *Y. pestis* and spread the plague. These fleas can live on rats, mice, squirrels, and chipmunks. Rats, particularly the black rat (*Rattus rattus*), are the primary zoonotic reservoirs (long-term animal carriers) of the plague. Rats are ideal reservoirs for *Y. pestis*. These rodents harbor both the bacteria and the fleas that carry them, and they live near human habitats. The rats live in large, dense populations, often in urban environments, which helps spread the bacteria among individual rats. Then when an infected rat dies, the fleas leave the body searching for new hosts, which are often nearby humans, thereby starting a human-to-human transmission chain.

This relationship between rats and humans in built-up areas was much more common in the past. In densely populated medieval cities, rats and humans lived in close quarters, allowing for the easy transfer of fleas and, by extension, the plague. Today, there are fewer rats in the cities as they are cleaner and have less food waste lying about.

THE THREE TYPES OF PLAGUE

Yersinia pestis can cause three types of plague: bubonic, pneumonic, and septicemic plague.

The bubonic form is the most common form of plague. It starts with a sudden onset of fever, chills, and headaches and is followed by dark, egg-sized blotches that ooze pus and bleed when opened. *Y. pestis* enters the victim's body through a flea bite and travels through the lymphatic system to the closest lymph node, where it multiplies. The lymph nodes become painful and swollen. The bubonic plague derives its name from the characteristic buboes, or swollen lymph nodes associated with the infection. The buboes typically develop in the groin, armpits, or neck. They are painful and can become so swollen that they are visible under the skin. Untreated, the infection can spread from the lymphatic system to the bloodstream or lungs, which can lead to the other forms of plague.

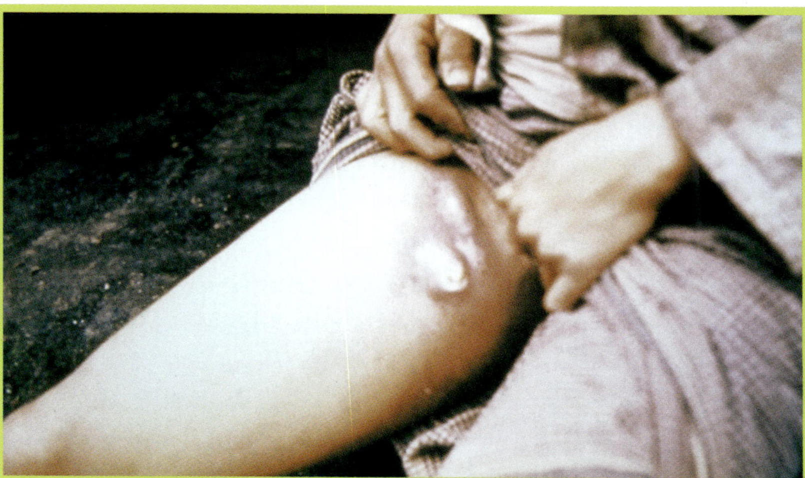

Buboes are a key characteristic of bubonic plague. As the infection advances, they can become so swollen that they burst.

Pneumonic plague occurs when *Y. pestis* infects the lungs. It is the only form of the disease that can spread from person to person through airborne droplets, expelled when the infected individual coughs out *Y. pestis* from their lungs. Symptoms include severe respiratory distress such as coughing, chest pain, difficulty breathing, and the production of a frothy, bloody sputum (mixture of spit and mucus). Pneumonic plague is often fatal, usually within twenty-four to forty-eight hours after symptoms start. During the Black Death, most bubonic plague infections progressed to the lungs and became a form of the coughing pneumonic plague.

Septicemic plague occurs when the infection spreads to the bloodstream. It can arise as a complication of bubonic or pneumonic plague or can occur on its own if the bacteria enter the bloodstream directly, bypassing the lymphatic system. This form of plague can cause sepsis, a life-threatening condition that can lead to tissue damage, organ failure, and death. Other symptoms include fever, chills, extreme weakness, abdominal pain, and shock, as well as gangrene (the blackening and death of tissue, most commonly on the fingers, toes, ears, and nose).

MAJOR PLAGUE PANDEMICS

There have been at least three plague pandemics. The first plague pandemic started in 541 BCE with the Plague of Justinian, which, in the next three centuries, crisscrossed the Mediterranean basin in at least fifteen successive waves of disease.

The second plague pandemic probably started in the Mongolian Steppe and traveled along the Silk Road through Eurasia. The second plague pandemic is often called the Black Death, and besides devastating the human population, it also sickened and killed dogs, cats, camels, and birds. The plague returned at varying intervals until the early nineteenth century CE, although it was never as deadly as the initial Black Death of the mid-1300s. In England, for example, the plague returned between 1360 and 1363, killing 20 percent of Londoners, and then again

ENDEMIC, EPIDEMIC, AND PANDEMIC

A disease outbreak is called a pandemic when it affects many people and rapidly expands its geographic range. Pandemics are usually caused by a new pathogen against which there is little or no preexisting immunity. Epidemics are similar but much more localized outbreaks than pandemics.

Pandemics and epidemics are new widespread outbreaks of diseases, while endemic diseases are constantly present at manageable levels. Endemic diseases such as malaria and the flu can become epidemics or even pandemics when the number of cases rises significantly above the expected number of cases, or they spread to new regions.

in 1369, killing another 10 to 15 percent.

In response to the second plague pandemic, people attempted various preventive measures. The use of masks, particularly by physicians, became common. Often filled with aromatic substances, these masks were based on the bad air theory. Physicians stuffed them with substances such as mint leaves, myrrh, rose petals, camphor, cloves, and straw to protect them from bad, foul-smelling air. The masks not only smelled good, but they unknowingly had the added benefit of preventing the transmission of airborne *Y. pestis* (pneumonic plague) through the mask.

Plague masks covered physicians' heads and had a hollow, beak-like structure in the front, allowing physicians to fill them with various substances. Physicians also often wore leather gloves and long coats to cover the rest of their bodies.

To prevent the spread of the Black Death, cities and nations took public health actions that, while rudimentary, laid the groundwork for modern epidemiology (the study of when and where diseases occur and how to control them). They imposed quarantines. For example, the Venetian-controlled port city of Ragusa (modern-day Dubrovnik, Croatia) was one of the first ports to implement a thirty-day isolation for ships and travelers. Public gatherings were banned, streets were cleaned, and in some cities, such as Milan, Italy, the houses of plague victims were walled up to contain the spread of the plague. Despite these efforts, the plague ravaged Europe, unchecked by the limited medical knowledge and public health infrastructure of the time.

The final plague pandemic is known as the third plague pandemic. It began in Yunnan, China, in 1855, and although it spread across all inhabited continents, it did most of its damage in Asia. Fifteen million people died in the third plague pandemic, with twelve million of the deaths occurring in China and India. The 1894 Hong Kong plague, during which the bacteria (*Yersinia pestis*) and the vector (fleas) responsible for the plague were discovered, was part of this pandemic.

The World Health Organization (WHO) declared the third plague pandemic over in 1960 when worldwide plague deaths dropped below two hundred a year. Since then, the number of plague fatalities has declined each year. The main reasons plague outbreaks ended are the increased sanitation of modern cities, which has limited the rat populations in urban areas, and the treatment of plague patients with antibiotics. But endemic bubonic plague is still found in the Democratic Republic of the Congo, Madagascar, and Peru.

Facing page: A timeline of various pandemics throughout history and estimates of how many deaths they caused. Scientists can make estimates, but it can be difficult to say exactly how many people died in historical pandemics (see sidebar on page 17).

A TIMELINE OF PANDEMICS AND THEIR ESTIMATED DEATH TOLLS

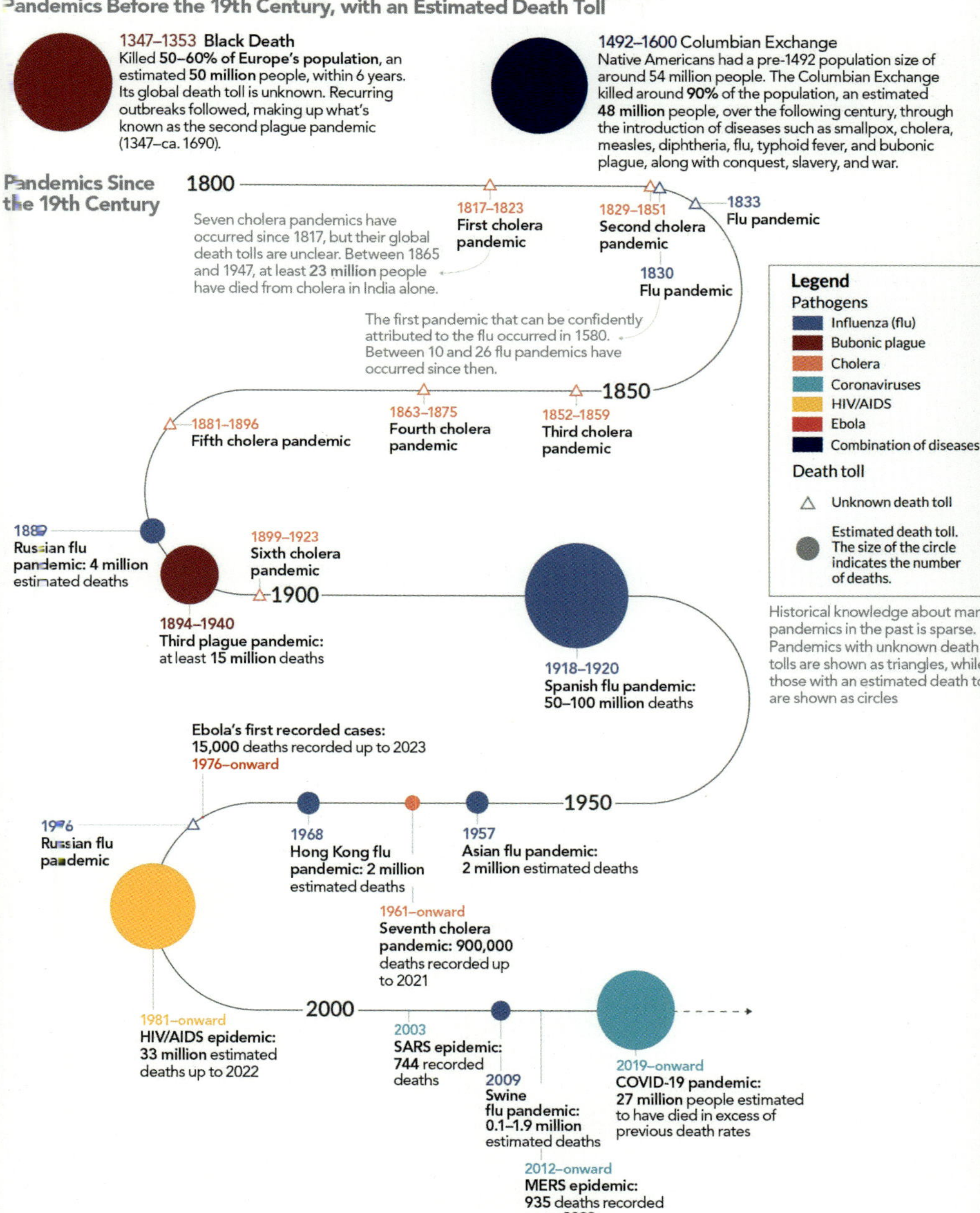

GENE SEQUENCING AND ANALYSIS

Common pathogens such as viruses, bacteria, and parasites contain genetic materials that provide the information to manufacture proteins, complex molecules that do most of the work in a cell, as well as new copies of themselves. This genetic material is called deoxyribonucleic acid (DNA) or ribonucleic acid (RNA) in some viruses. The order—or sequence—of the nucleotide bases that make up a virus's DNA (or its RNA equivalent) encode this information. DNA has four nucleotide bases: adenine (A), thymine (T), cytosine (C), and guanine (G). RNA also has four bases, but it uses uracil (U) in place of thymine. Genomic sequencing technologies can determine the order of nucleotide bases in a pathogen's genetic material.

We can think of the genetic material of a pathogen as its recipe book to make proteins. If we look at the order of the letters (the order of the nucleotide bases in genetic material) that make up the recipe (gene for a protein), we can read the recipe and understand it. The whole recipe book is the sum of all the recipes, as the genome is the sum of all the genes. If we know the sequence of all the letters in a recipe book, then we know all the recipes. And if we know the sequence of all the nucleotide bases in the genome, then we know all the genes.

When a new disease is found, one of the first things researchers do is determine the nucleotide sequence. This is called sequencing the pathogen. For example, within a few weeks of the first COVID-19 case, researchers sequenced the virus causing the disease, establishing its similarity to the SARS virus, which we'll talk about more in chapter 5. Knowing the nucleotide sequence of a new pathogen is incredibly useful in finding its relationship to other known pathogens.

Pathogens evolve when the enzyme that copies their genetic material makes errors as the pathogen replicates. These errors are called mutations. In some mutations, nucleotide bases can be added or deleted, or one nucleotide can be replaced with another. (This would be like making mistakes when copying the recipe book.) The lifespan of pathogens is short. They replicate quickly and produce large numbers of new pathogens. Most mutations do not affect the pathogen's efficiency, but some might increase its infectiousness or allow it to avoid its host's immune system. Such mutations result in the pathogens with these mutations becoming more common in future generations. We can observe these changes by sequencing pathogens in different people at varying times and places and comparing the similarity of the sequences. Infections with similar sequences come from the same geographic region and period. So using sequence analysis, researchers can determine where and when an infection originated or entered a particular area. The recipe book analogy still holds. By carefully reading recipe books, we can determine which countries they are from and when they were written. Recipes also evolve to match changing tastes.

Sequences of genetic materials of pathogens in different organisms (such as sequences in bats versus civets versus cats) can establish whether each organism or species is infected by the same virus and how similar the pathogen sequence is to that found in humans. Researchers use computers to determine the sequence of the common ancestor of a pathogen in humans. If that sequence is identical or nearly identical to the sequence of the same pathogen in another species, that species could be the original host of the pathogen.

Since 2010, sequencing techniques have continually improved. Scientists can isolate and analyze DNA fragments in bone and tooth pulp from tens of thousands of years ago and then use advanced sequence analyses to distinguish the pathogen nucleotide sequences from other DNA contaminants, such as insects. They can determine the genome of ancient pathogens and gather information from incredibly early pandemics. In essence, we can study a molecular fossil record of microbial evolution.

UNDERSTANDING HOW THE PLAGUE EVOLVED

Scientists have been applying advanced sequence analysis to study plague bacteria. By sequencing genomes from skeletal remains found across Eurasia, scientists traced the evolutionary trajectory of *Yersinia pestis*. This research revealed that the genomic sequences of *Y. pestis* diverged from a common ancestor infecting humans about fifty-seven hundred years ago. These findings underscore how ancient DNA studies illuminate the origins and adaptations of pathogens over time. But confirming these evolutionary patterns requires interdisciplinary collaboration—archaeologists, paleoclimatologists (scientists who study ancient climates), and historians must work alongside geneticists. This helps geneticists understand and contextualize genomic data within broader historical and environmental frameworks.

In one such interdisciplinary study, researchers showed that *Y. pestis* found in Kyrgyzstan graves are the direct bacterial ancestors of those that triggered the Black Death. The story started with Philip Slavin, a historian specializing in economic and environmental issues at the University of Stirling in the United Kingdom. He discovered archival records from two fourteenth-century graveyards in Kyrgyzstan. These graveyards stood out to him due to the high number of gravestones from 1338 and 1339, with several tombstones explicitly mentioning a pandemic.

To explore any connections these burials might have had to the Black Death, Slavin hunted down the skeletal remains of seven individuals associated with the gravestones and passed them onto Maria Spyrou, an archaeogeneticist (a scientist who studies ancient DNA from archaeological remains such as skeletons) at the University of Tübingen in Germany. Spyrou then led a team that extracted and sequenced ancient DNA from the seven skeletons. She found *Y. pestis* DNA in three of them. The genetic analysis of the DNA revealed that these strains of *Y. pestis* were precursors of the *Y. pestis* associated with the Black Death, and they were also the ancestors of the modern *Y. pestis* lineages that are still around.

THE HISTORY OF PANDEMICS

Because there are conflicting definitions distinguishing epidemics from pandemics and because it is challenging to determine how many people died from disease outbreaks that occurred centuries ago, there is no standard list of pandemics throughout history—the lists all differ a little. Still, they have some similarities. The Black Death, smallpox, and the 1918 flu were the worst pandemics in recorded history and appear on all lists. There have been numerous plague outbreaks. And modern pandemics have lower death tolls than those occurring before industrialization began in the late 1700s.

But one major disease outbreak often doesn't make the list. The so-called Columbian Exchange is one of the largest and most historically important disease outbreaks but is not classified as a pandemic by many. When Christopher Columbus's 1492 expedition reached the Americas, about 54 million Native Americans lived on the land. By 1600 the population had decreased to just 5.6 million, representing a decrease as high as 90 percent. Most of the deaths were due to widespread conflict, enslavement, and the introduction of numerous fatal diseases including smallpox, cholera, diphtheria, influenza, typhoid fever, and measles. These diseases had a particularly devastating effect on Native Americans, who had never encountered these diseases before and had no immunity to them. But many people don't consider the Columbian Exchange a pandemic because it was caused not by a single disease but by a series of diseases new to the Americas. Regardless of classification, this event represents one of the greatest demographic catastrophes in human history, with a mortality rate far exceeding most official pandemics.

Through this study, researchers not only learned about the origin of the Black Death but also how the plague bacteria spread. Artifacts found in the Kyrgyz graves included pearls from the Indian Ocean, Mediterranean corals, and various foreign coins, suggesting that the region hosted considerable trade activity. Slavin proposes that such extensive trade was pivotal in the westward spread of the plague.

EXTERNAL FACTORS RESPONSIBLE FOR PLAGUE PANDEMICS

The bacteria that cause the plague, the fleas that carry the bacteria, and the rats that host the infected fleas have been around for thousands of years. Yet the plague comes in waves, and plague pandemics are extremely rare. That is because several prerequisites are necessary for a global disease outbreak to occur. What are they, and why was the Black Death so deadly? Why did it kill half the Eurasian population in just four years?

The remains of the genetic material of the plague bacteria, *Y. pestis*, isolated from mid-sixth-century skeletons found in burial grounds in England, Germany, and Spain showed that sometime between the Bronze Age (3000 BCE–1000 CE) and the fifth century CE, the virus responsible for the plague had mutated so that *Y. pestis* could survive, and even thrive, in fleas. So, in all the plague outbreaks before the fifth century, the plague spread from person to person. It was a purely respiratory disease—there was no bubonic plague, just pneumonic and septicemic plagues. But from the Plague of Justinian onward, *Y. pestis* were not just spread through coughing and sneezing. They could be injected right into the lymphatic system by the bite of an infected flea. The plague had evolved into a deadlier, more infectious form. The Plague of Justinian still wasn't as lethal or widespread as the Black Death, although historical records of buboes on victims confirm they were experiencing the newly evolved bubonic plague. Why was the Black Death so much deadlier?

The reasons are complex and multifaceted. More than just an evolutionary adaptation of the disease, joint biological, environmental, social, and economic factors created conditions ripe for the emergence and spread of a super deadly plague.

In the fourteenth century, the global climate changed due to the onset of the Little Ice Age. It started with a massive volcanic eruption on one of the Indonesian islands. It released so much ash into the atmosphere that it blocked the sun. Summer disappeared, and crops died. This caused the black rat population to migrate from the increasingly colder, desolated regions of central Asia to the warmer,

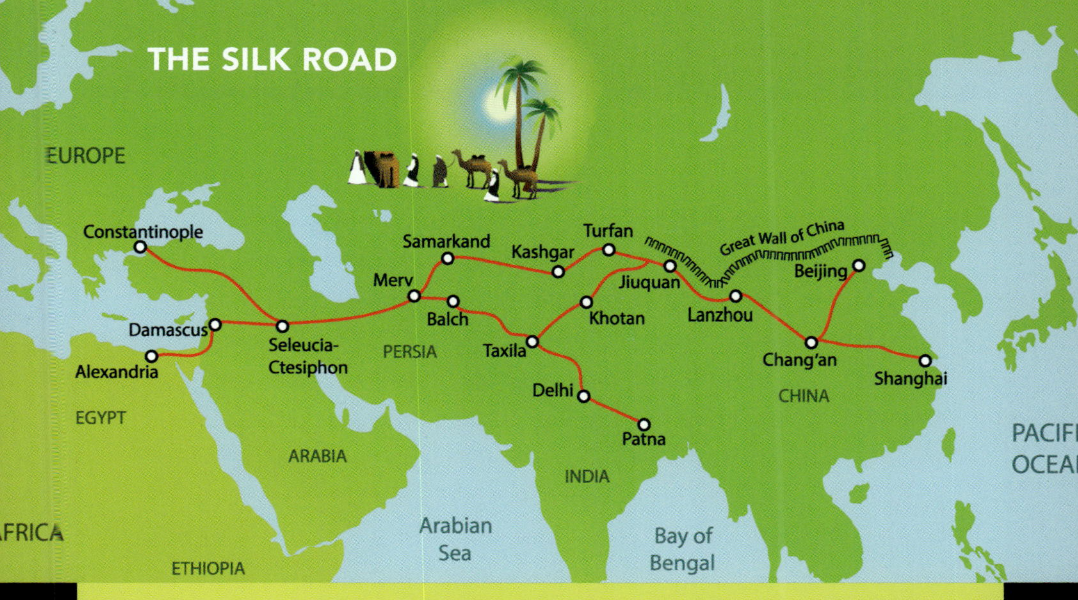

The Silk Road was a network of trade routes stretching about 4,000 miles (6,437 km) from China to Italy. It allowed people in Asia, the Middle East, and Europe to swap goods and ideas.

more populated southern areas of central and East Asia. The Black Death started there. Infected black rats moved into large towns and cities with people living in close quarters in squalor and dirt, conditions that suited the black rats. It was also where the rats encountered the Silk Road trade routes.

The Mongol Empire had just expanded across Asia, creating a vast territory that united many regions under a single political structure, allowing for more movement of peoples and goods and, by extension, pathogens. Normally, rats have a fairly limited range. Without ecological stressors, they travel just a few miles in their whole lives. But the Mongols started trading and traveling all over Eurasia, creating the Silk Road and inadvertently offering the rats a ride and dramatically expanding their reach.

Black rats and their fleas thrived in the cramped and unhygienic conditions of the merchant caravans and ships on the trade route, which transported the plague across continents. By road and sea, the plague-ridden rats spread the Black Death to every corner of the Silk Road. Due to the slow pace of medieval travel, which would have been no faster than a horse or ship travels, and the enormity of Eurasia, it took months to travel from China to Crimea. The spread of the plague was correspondingly slow—it took years to spread from its origins on the Mongolian Steppe, along the Silk Road, to Europe via Crimea. It was a slow but steady spread.

The pandemic's acceleration is possibly linked to a Mongolian siege of the Genoese (Italian) trading post at the city of Kaffa (now Feodosia) in Crimea. In 1346, while the Mongols were waiting for the besieged Genoese to surrender, they became terribly ill—the Black Death had caught up with them. Struggling with rapidly diminishing and sickening forces, the Mongol commanders had one final move. In an early instance of biological warfare, they catapulted the infected corpses of their comrades over the Kaffa city walls. The beleaguered Genoese inside the fort soon fell ill with the plague. In panic, they scrambled aboard their ships and fled Crimea, back toward Italy—to Genoa, Venice, and other Mediterranean ports, from where the plague spread like wildfire throughout the rest of Europe. They were carrying with them the very plague they sought to escape.

Besides the Little Ice Age causing a black rat migration to the Silk Road and the siege of Kaffa spreading *Y. pestis* from the Mongols to the Genoese traders, there was one more prerequisite for the plague to explode into the Black Death. The disease-carrying fleas needed a reason to jump from black rats to humans. Fleas prefer living and getting their blood meals from rats rather than from humans. The rat population had to be stressed for fleas to jump to humans. During the thirteenth and fourteenth centuries, a civil war in China led to episodes of widespread famine, driving starving black rats into towns and cities to find food without much success. The fleas jumped from the malnourished and cold black rats to slightly healthier humans. Things were no better in Europe, where the Great Famine of the fourteenth century resulted in hunger and malnutrition for rats and humans. Typically, a rat only carries five to ten fleas, but during a famine, when rats starve and become rare, the surviving rodents often carry a couple of hundred fleas each.

In both Europe and Asia, the growth of medieval cities, poor sanitation (medieval Europeans rarely washed or changed their clothes more than once a year), and overcrowded living conditions facilitated the spread of the disease. It allowed the hungry, malnourished rats to move into the urban centers, where their proximity allowed the fleas (vectors) to jump from the rats (the reservoirs) to the humans (hosts). The medieval cities also provided the population density required to keep the chain of infection going. About four hundred thousand people were needed for the infection to sustain itself in human populations. Without at least four hundred thousand people, the last infectious individual recovers or dies before reaching another susceptible individual, so the pathogen locally disappears. The pathogen can't keep an uninterrupted chain of transmission going, and plague outbreaks become sporadic events instead of epidemics or pandemics.

LOOKING BACK AT THE PLAGUE

We can learn a lot about modern infectious diseases from the Black Death. Although the second plague pandemic occurred in the Middle Ages, which was a long time ago, it was a slow-motion preview of the diseases without borders we find in our globalized and highly mobile world. Without understanding why it was beneficial, physicians used masks, quarantines, and isolations to prevent the spread of the plague, methods that are still used to combat illnesses such as COVID-19. Furthermore, in examining the causes of the Black Death, we have been introduced to several driving forces that are still initiating new outbreaks of modern diseases. Historically, these include urbanization (rats in cities), travel (movement from the Mongolian Steppe to Eurasia), climate change (Little Ice Age), ecological stress (drove black rats to Silk Road), politics (open movement along Silk Road), conflicts (Crimean siege), and misinformation (flagellation and bad air theory).

Numerous pandemics, epidemics, and disease outbreaks have occurred between the plague and COVID-19 pandemics. There is so much we can learn about modern and future diseases from them.

CHAPTER 2

THE 1918 FLU AND HUMAN MOBILIZATION

HUMAN MOBILIZATION

The vast network of human connections that modern transport allows, and global population growth, has increased interactions between people, creating an unprecedented potential for infectious diseases to spread. Each jet-setting traveler may act as a conduit for pathogens, ferrying viruses and bacteria across national and international borders. Meanwhile, inequities in the world economy have led to increased migrations across country borders, which may also contribute to the spreading of infectious diseases. Commercial transport of animals and accidental stowaways such as rodents on ships and insects aboard aircraft can create additional pathways for spreading diseases since these stowaways may carry illnesses with them. These scenarios have significantly increased the probability of infectious outbreaks evolving into pandemics, compared to the era before such extensive contact and travel became possible. And they continue multiplying, driven by a global economy that is highly dependent on the flow of goods across oceans and through the skies.

The international transport industry has witnessed a meteoric rise since industrialization. The distances over which people and products are transported have surged. Centralized transport hubs, such as the bustling ports of Shanghai, China; Singapore; and Rotterdam, Netherlands, and major airports such as those in Atlanta, Georgia; Dubai, United Arab Emirates; and Tokyo, Japan, have become unavoidable for international trade. The number of people traveling through these hubs is also astronomical. For instance, Atlanta's airport, the world's busiest airport, served 104.7 million passengers in 2023. These travel hubs are convenient and efficient. But they also are conduits for the rapid transmission of diseases across the globe. In our global transport network, no place remains distant. An outbreak in the farthest corner of the world can be transported to many cities in less than a day, making the concept of isolation obsolete. Local health incidents can morph into global emergencies at breakneck speed.

This chapter introduces the 1918 influenza pandemic, demonstrating how international travel has facilitated the spread of diseases, enabling localized outbreaks to escalate into global pandemics. To begin, it is essential to understand the nature of influenza viruses and how they work.

BASICS OF INFLUENZA

While it's widely believed that touching contaminated surfaces such as doorknobs is a common flu transmission route, actual infection in this manner is relatively uncommon. The influenza virus is predominantly spread through aerosolized droplets released by sneezing. A powerful sneeze, capable of bringing tears to the eyes and echoing through a room, can send up to forty thousand droplets hurtling at speeds reaching 200 miles (322 km) per hour, each potentially carrying one hundred million flu viruses. Flu viruses are also emitted when an infected person talks or coughs. The larger droplets settle quickly, but the smaller ones can float in the air for days.

Flu symptoms are similar to but more intense than those of a common cold. They can range from fever and cough to muscle aches,

VIRUSES

Influenza is caused by a virus, not bacteria. Viruses are submicroscopic pathogens. They are so small that they can't be seen with a light microscope, which is why they were discovered two hundred years after bacteria. The first human virus to be discovered was the yellow fever virus in 1901. Researchers determined that mosquitoes transmit yellow fever and that the disease agent had to be a filterable, blood-borne entity smaller than bacteria—a virus. But it was only after the invention of the electron microscope in 1931 that scientists saw a virus for the first time, the tobacco mosaic virus, which infects various plant species.

Viruses are parasites—they must inhabit host cells to make thousands of copies of themselves. They can infect all types of living organisms, from humans and animals to plants to even bacteria and fungi. They exist in all of Earth's ecosystems, whether terrestrial, underground, underwater, or airborne, and are the most abundant biological entities.

The small size and simplicity of viruses allow them to evade the body's defense mechanisms and make them more mobile. Bacteria, such as *Y. pestis*, are much larger than viruses and, therefore, require much larger droplets for transmission from person to person. These large droplets are much rarer because they fall out of the air faster due to gravity and therefore travel shorter distances and are less likely to pass through the upper respiratory system than the small particles. Large particles get caught in nose hairs, and sneezes and coughs expel them. So, in comparison to viral infections such as the flu, bacterial infections such as the pneumonic plague are not as contagious.

headaches, and general fatigue, varying in intensity depending on the strain of the flu virus involved. The flu can also be fatal. Between 1976 and 2017, the United States saw annual flu-related deaths from as few as three thousand to as many as eighty thousand. Those at higher risk of severe complications from the flu include older adults, young children, pregnant people, and individuals with chronic conditions such as asthma. Flu epidemics and pandemics are challenging to slow down because 50 percent of infected individuals exhibit no symptoms

There are about 10^{31} (10 with 31 zeros after it) viruses on Earth. They can be divided into about 10^9 species, fewer than 250 of which are known to infect humans. Although they are parasites, most viruses don't cause human diseases. Many play a vital role in controlling the number and diversity of bacteria in our bodies.

Unlike bacteria and eukaryotes (any organism made of one or more cells with a clear nucleus), viruses are not made of cells. By themselves, viruses are inert (lifeless) objects composed of genetic material (DNA or RNA), a protein shell (capsid), and sometimes a lipid envelope. Viruses only contain DNA or RNA—not both. But this genetic material contains all the information necessary to make a new virus. The life cycle of all viruses is similar. They come to "life" once they infect their host and force the host to use their own cellular machinery to make millions of new viruses using the instructions from the virus's genetic material. Each new virus can then break out of the host cell and find a new host cell. This often kills the host cells.

Viruses spread in many different ways. They can be carried by vectors, such as insects carrying plant diseases or bloodsucking bugs carrying animal diseases. Airborne transmission occurs via respiratory droplets, as seen with flu viruses and SARS-CoV-2 (the virus that causes COVID-19). Others, such as norovirus and rotavirus, spread through contaminated hands, food, or water. Human immunodeficiency virus (HIV) is spread through sexual contact or blood.

but are still contagious and because patients who get sick are contagious before they feel sick.

The impact of the flu extends far beyond its physical symptoms. In the United States, it is estimated that each year, influenza outbreaks are responsible for about 3.1 million days of inpatient hospitalization and 31.4 million outpatient hospital visits. The direct medical costs attributed to the flu average $10.4 billion annually. Still, these figures are insignificant compared to the human and financial toll of a widespread flu pandemic.

CATEGORIZING INFLUENZA

The three main types of human influenza viruses are A, B, and C. They are also divided into many subtypes. Two surface glycoproteins distinguish the subtypes of influenzas A and B: hemagglutinin (H) and neuraminidase (N). Glycoproteins are biomolecules (molecules produced by living organisms) that are found on the surface of viruses. They are made up of sugars (glyco) and proteins. The A and B flu viruses have N and H glycoproteins. The C type, which is much less clinically significant, doesn't.

The H glycoproteins help the virus enter human host cells by finding and binding to receptors on the surface of the cells. When they enter the host cell, the viral envelope (the outermost layer of many viruses) dissolves and releases the viral genetic material inside it into the cell. Inside the cell, the virus's eight genes are replicated and used to assemble new influenza viruses. This rapid replication of the viral genes often results in errors, leading to a high mutation rate and the evolution of diverse viral strains, some more severe than others. Within a mere ten hours after infection, each host cell can produce between one hundred thousand and one million copies of the infecting virus, including the more severe strains. The N glycoproteins then aid in releasing new viruses from infected cells.

Influenza A viruses, which also cause the flu in birds and nonhuman mammals such as pigs, have caused all known influenza pandemics in humans. More than 130 different subtypes of influenza A have been observed in animals, and they are named for which subtypes of H and N glycoproteins they carry. There are eighteen known H subtypes and eleven N subtypes of influenza A. Most varieties are found only in birds, but the H1, H2, H3, N1, and N2 subtypes are common in humans. H1N1 and H3N2 are the most common subtypes circulating among humans.

Naming strains of influenza A is not extremely complicated. The 2009 pandemic virus is identified as the 2009 H1N1 Mexican swine flu pandemic, an H1N1 subtype. It was originally isolated in

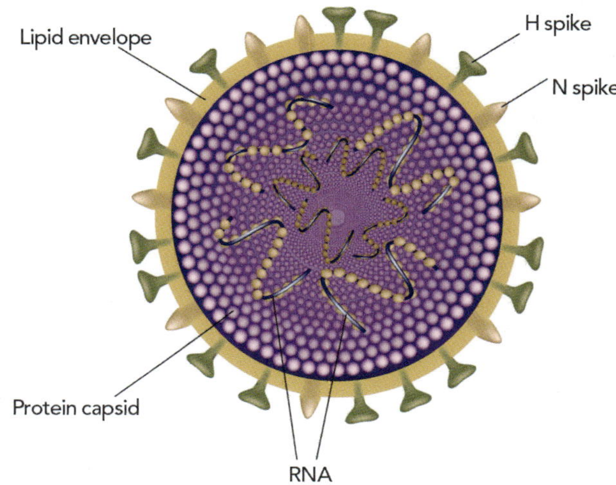

A flu virus consists of genetic material (RNA) housed in a protective protein capsid. A lipid envelope surrounds the capsid, from which the H and N glycoproteins protrude.

Mexico and initially circulated among pigs (swine) before crossing over into humans.

Although the influenza A and B viruses cause similar symptoms, influenza B only infects humans and seals and has never caused a pandemic. Influenza C is the mildest form of influenza. It typically only causes minor upper respiratory illnesses and rarely results in severe health consequences in humans.

HOW FLU VIRUSES EVADE THE IMMUNE SYSTEM

When someone gets sick, specialized white blood cells notice the pathogens and activate the immune system. If the body overcomes the pathogens, white blood cells remember the germs so that next time they can fight the pathogens off quicker, often before the person feels sick again. This is also how some vaccines, including the flu vaccine, work. By exposing white blood cells to a harmless or weakened form of the virus, the immune system learns to recognize and respond more effectively to the actual virus if encountered in the future.

White blood cells only identify specific parts of pathogens, called antigens. For the flu virus, the main antigens are the H and N glycoproteins that protrude from the outside of the virus. When two flu viruses' antigens are similar, a host's immune response—learned from infection or vaccination with one of the viruses—will recognize and neutralize the other virus, thereby protecting the host against the other virus too. To avoid detection, influenza viruses have evolved so that the genes for H and N mutate faster than any of their other genes, resulting in new viral generations with antigens that a host's immune system can't recognize.

Flu viruses have another trick: Their genes are divided into separate pieces, unlike most viruses, which have their genes in single, continuous segments. If two different flu viruses enter the same cell, they can mix up their pieces and create a new hybrid virus. This mixing of gene fragments, called reassortment, allows the influenza virus to mutate much faster than other viruses. For instance, pigs can get sick with flu viruses from both birds and humans. If a pig gets both kinds simultaneously, the viruses can swap pieces, creating a new bird flu virus that can make people sick too. Most of the time, the mixed and mutant genes aren't functional, or if they do work, they are no more effective than the original genes. With so many viruses in an infected pig and how quickly they multiply, if just one in a million mutations resulted in an improved virus, soon there would be hundreds of thousands of new copies of that improved virus.

What might reassortment mean for people? Usually, the H1N1 swine flu virus can spread between people, but it doesn't cause many fatalities. The 2009 H1N1 Mexican swine flu infected over two billion people, but fewer than 0.1 percent of them died. Variants of that strain are still circulating. But the H5N1 bird flu virus is very deadly when it infects humans. It has a fatality rate greater than 50 percent. That is higher than the plague, which had the highest fatality of all pandemics.

VIRAL REASSORTMENT

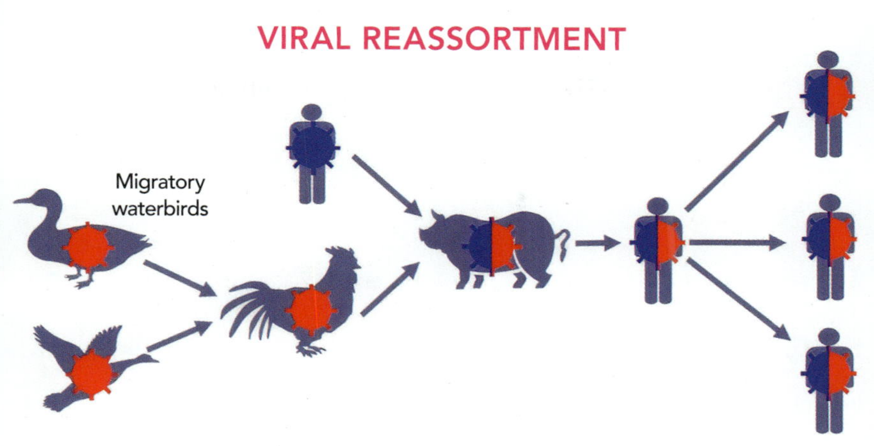

This diagram shows how a pig can act as a mixing vessel for flu viruses. When an avian flu virus from a bird (red) and a human flu virus (blue) infect a pig at the same time, their genes can shuffle together. This creates a dangerous new hybrid virus (red and blue) that is capable of both infecting humans and spreading easily from person to person.

Fortunately, H5N1 does not spread easily from person to person and rarely crosses from bird to person. But epidemiologists and virologists (scientists who study viruses) are worried about the possible mutation and outbreak of either a hybrid swine flu virus (H1N1) that would have an increased mortality rate due to some bird flu (H5N1) gene fragments being incorporated or an avian flu hybrid with increased transmissibility obtained from the swine flu virus.

ADAPTING FLU VACCINES TO GLOBAL SEASONAL TRENDS

In temperate climates, influenza outbreaks are associated with cold weather and indoor living, while in tropical regions, influenza may occur throughout the year, causing outbreaks more irregularly. In the United States, the flu season starts in October and peaks in February. In summer the incidence (frequency) of flu cases drops but does not disappear.

THE REPRODUCTIVE NUMBER AND EXCESS MORTALITY

THE BASIC REPRODUCTIVE NUMBER (R_0)

The basic reproductive number gives us a good idea of how infectious a pathogen is. It is the number of people one person infects if the surrounding population has no previous immunity or hasn't been vaccinated.

The number of infected patients will grow if the average patient infects more than one other individual—that is, if R_0 is greater than one. If R_0 is less than one, the disease will die out. The value of R_0 is not a well-defined disease-specific constant. It depends on many variables, such as the behavior of the people (do they stay indoors and use masks?) and what strain of the pathogen is being evaluated (the ancestral variant of COVID-19 has a R_0 of 2.9, while the omicron variant has a R_0 of 9.5).

Measles has the highest reproduction number of all common infectious diseases, with an R_0 of 14. That means in the absence of vaccinations, quarantines, and isolation, the average patient will infect fourteen new people, who will typically each pass the disease onto fourteen new victims. One goes to fourteen, who all together infect 196 (14^2), and 196 infect 2,744 (14^3). After just five multiplications, we get half a million people with measles, and after two more rounds of infection, everyone in the world would be infected. But most people are vaccinated against measles. An R_0 of 14 is extreme, but it is a good example of how reproductive numbers illustrate the exponential

Due to continual mutations, a new subtype of the influenza virus becomes dominant during flu season each year. In response, the World Health Organization recommends updated vaccine formulations annually to protect against the variant they predict will spread. The WHO also tailors different vaccine formulations for the Northern and Southern Hemispheres to match their seasonal patterns. The vaccines are designed to protect patients against viruses known to cause growth of infectious diseases. At first, they grow slowly, and then their growth explodes.

EXCESS MORTALITY

Excess mortality or excess death analysis is a well-established method that scientists have used for centuries to estimate and compare the death tolls of disease outbreaks. It is the difference between observed and expected deaths for a set period, and it is often reported as a percentage of the number of expected deaths. Here is how they calculate it:

$$\text{Excess mortality (\%)} = \frac{\text{(Actual deaths} - \text{Expected deaths)}}{\text{Expected deaths}} \times 100$$

Excess mortality allows epidemiologists to compare epidemics that have occurred during different periods (for example, the 1918 influenza versus COVID-19) or countries (COVID-19 in the United States versus India), in which there have been variations in the way deaths have been recorded, the way the causes of deaths have been determined, and medical knowledge. Determination of excess mortality requires knowledge of the total number of fatalities expected based on previous observations and the number of deaths that occur during the epidemic. The measure considers both the direct deaths caused by the disease and the indirect deaths caused by factors such as disruptions to health-care services and the supply chain.

influenza epidemics. Typically, the vaccines are based on one influenza A (H1N1) virus, one influenza A (H3N2) virus, and two influenza B viruses.

THE 1918 FLU

The Black Death took several years to spread from the Mongolian Steppes to Europe. Influenza can circle the world in less than a month.

The 1918 flu pandemic illustrates this rapid spread. There are two primary reasons why influenza can spread much faster than the plague. First, the transmission of *Yersinia pestis* to and between humans is complicated as it involves a transfer from fleas to rats and, ultimately, fleas to humans. The flu is passed directly from person to person. Second, the 1918 flu spread much faster than the medieval plague due to the increased speed and volume of human travel in 1918 compared to 1345. During the Black Death, only traders and soldiers traveled, and both they and the infected rats that spread the plague could journey no faster than the swiftest forms of transport available—horses and ships. Ship travel was too slow to spread infectious diseases to new regions. Infected individuals on board ships often either died or recovered from their disease before reaching a new port. Six hundred years later, trains and steamships transported travelers and their germs across great distances at great speed, propelling the flu along with them.

In 1918 the harshest winter on record in the Midwest of the United States, coupled with the extensive movement of people due to World War I (1914–1918), set the stage for the deadliest flu pandemic in history. Cold temperatures meant people spent more time indoors, where the flu viruses spread between them. Across the United States, military camps overflowed with draftees who were crammed into spaces much too small for their numbers. New recruits came from all over the United States, to complete their training and leave for combat stations across the globe. Workers flocked to new factories opened for wartime production, where they shared overcrowded living spaces. The stage was set for a flu outbreak that would kill more people than the combined combat deaths of World War I, World War II (1939–1945), the Korean War (1950–1953), and the Vietnam War (1954–1975).

The 1918 flu pandemic probably began in Camp Funston, Kansas, where the overcrowded living quarters in army camps contributed to the rapid spread of the disease. The first flu case emerged on March 4, and within three weeks, over a thousand soldiers needed hospital

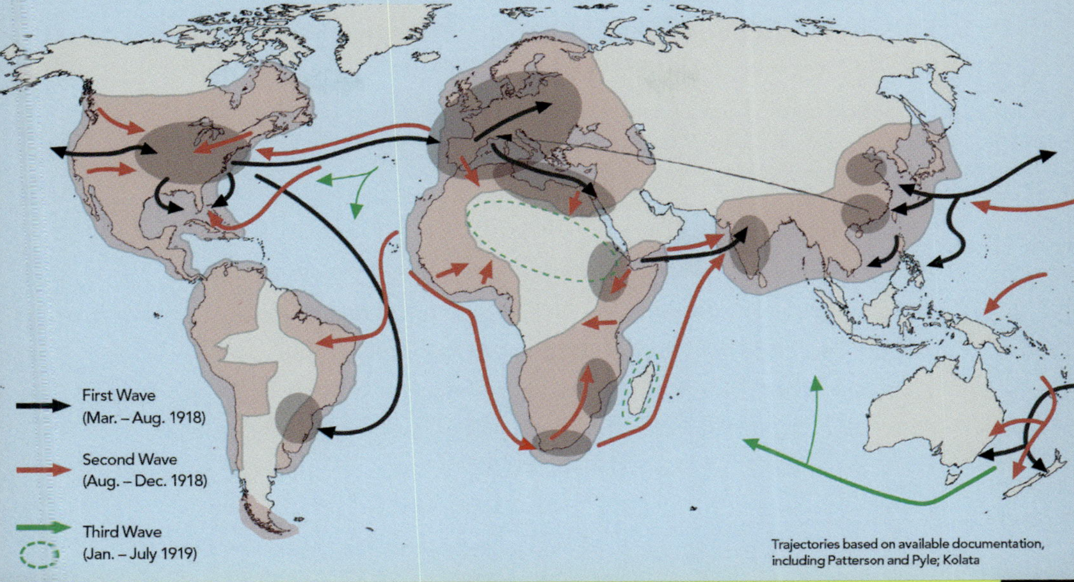

A map of the global routes of the first (black), second (red), and third (green) waves of the 1918 flu pandemic.

care. Just a month later, it had spread to thirty major US cities, most of which were near military bases. As US soldiers were deployed to Europe, they brought the flu virus to England, Spain, and France. The disease even jumped across the battle lines and infected the Germans.

Spain was neutral in World War I and, therefore, was more truthful in its accounting of influenza fatalities. In May 1918, eight million people died in Spain due to the flu. This resulted in Spain mistakenly (or conveniently for the United States) being thought of as the pandemic's origin and the pandemic being named the Spanish flu, which many people still call it.

There were three distinct onslaughts of the pandemic: the initial wave in spring and two more virulent waves in the fall and winter of 1918. The later waves brought severe symptoms, causing such violent coughing and sneezing that some patients suffered from torn lungs and burst eardrums, in addition to bleeding from various body parts, hallucinations, and extreme oxygen deprivation that turned the patient's extremities blue and black. The 1918 flu was highly contagious, and it killed quickly. Many victims died less than twelve hours after exhibiting the first symptoms.

Although the Black Death killed a larger percentage of the total population, the 1918 influenza pandemic claimed more lives in one year than the Black Death did in a century. About one-third of the world's population experienced flu symptoms during the outbreak, and the death toll was fifty million to one hundred million people. The majority of those who died were in the prime of their lives. For some reason, the 1918 flu virus targeted healthy young adults instead of the usual high-risk groups such as children, older adults, and pregnant people.

During the pandemic, neither scientists nor medical researchers realized that a virus was responsible for the influenza outbreak—viruses had just been discovered. Nearly ten years after the flu had run its course, virologists isolated two closely related influenza viruses (now known to be H1N1 viruses) from humans and pigs and showed that they were responsible for the 1918 pandemic.

Even more information came later from an Alaskan village named Brevig Mission. The 1918 flu claimed the lives of seventy-two out of its eighty inhabitants. All the victims were buried in the permafrost, including a woman in her thirties whose body fat protected her lung tissue from decomposing. In 2005 researchers used her preserved lung tissues to isolate fragments of influenza virus genetic material, which they used to sequence the 1918 flu virus's genome. Their findings suggested that the virus originated in birds and then crossed into mammals sometime between 1880 and 1912. While researchers still debate whether it first infected pigs and then humans or crossed from birds to humans, clearly, the virus originated from an avian source.

The genetic information didn't reveal why the 1918 flu was so severe or why it mainly affected young adults. But in 2007, experiments with genetically reconstructed versions of the virus and studies using animal models provided some insights into its severity. The 1918 flu was devastating because it caused an overreaction of the immune system. This overreaction damaged the lungs in animals, mirroring the extensive lung damage seen in human victims of the pandemic.

OTHER INFLUENZA PANDEMICS

Since 1900 there have been four flu pandemics. The latest occurred in 2009. Initially, it was called the swine flu pandemic due to its prevalence in pig populations before human transmission. Now it is called the H1N1/09 influenza or 2009 H1N1 Mexican swine flu. The first signs of the 2009 influenza emerged in Mexico on March 28, 2009. The virus was highly infectious, and within five months, it had spread to an estimated fifty million individuals globally, prompting

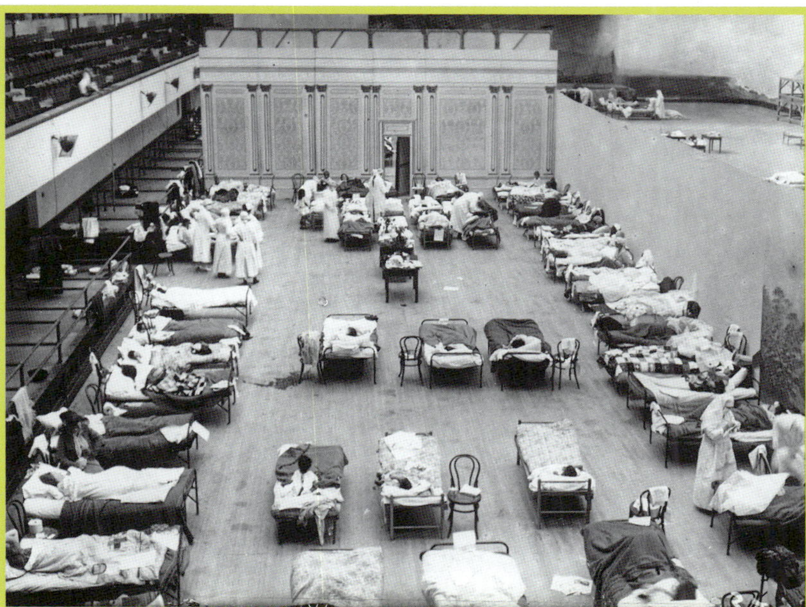

The 1918 flu pandemic was so severe that people often had to turn public spaces, such as this auditorium in Oakland, California, into makeshift hospitals to house the rapid increase of patients.

the WHO to declare it a pandemic. The pandemic, while extensive, exhibited a low mortality rate, with fewer than one in a thousand infections resulting in death. Neither it nor other flu pandemics approached the 1918 pandemic in severity or mortality rates.

INFLUENZA AND COVID-19 OUTBREAKS AMONG HUMANS FROM 1900 TO NOW

OUTBREAKS/ PANDEMICS	NUMBER INFECTED	DEATHS	CASE FATALITY RATE (%)
1918 (H1N1)	~500 million	~50 million	2.5–10
1957 Asian flu (H2N2)	~500 million	1–4 million	<0.2
1968 Hong Kong flu (H3N2)	~500 million	1–4 million	<0.2
2009 swine flu (H1N1)	~60 million	~15,000	<0.1
SEASONAL FLU			
Seasonal flu	~100 million	~50,000	<0.1
BIRD FLU			
2006 avian flu (H5N1)	115	79	~60
COVID-19			
COVID-19 (SARS-CoV-2)	778 million	7.1 million	1–14

MIGHT WE SEE ANOTHER FLU PANDEMIC?

Thanks to advanced knowledge, medications, and surveillance systems, the world is better equipped to deal with a spillover (zoonotic disease transmission) of the avian flu than it was in 1918. Many modern factors promote the spread of flu viruses, including increased travel, population density, and large-scale poultry and swine farms that can act as viral mixing bowls. For example, in 2022, chicken was the most consumed meat in the United States. The average person ate 98.8 pounds (44.8 kg) a year of chicken, up from 84.2 pounds (38.1 kg) in 2004.

When chickens live in large, crowded quarters on poultry farms, it's much easier for them to spread bird flu among one another and to other animals on the farm, such as pigs.

This increase in chicken consumption and an ever-growing population has led to the rise of massive poultry farms that typically house about half a million chickens, although some have more than fifteen million birds in one facility. The number and size of large-scale pig farms have grown just as much. The large, dense populations of pigs and chickens have created conditions suited for accelerated virus evolution by reassortment and rapid virus transmission.

Birds present a unique threat as a potential source for future influenza pandemics. Researchers have shown that just five mutations are required to transform the H5N1 avian virus into a form that can be spread from person to person by coughs and sneezes. Two of the five mutations have been found in some wild birds. The bird flu virus also behaves differently in birds than when it has crossed over into humans. In birds, the flu affects the digestive system as well as the lungs, which means bird poop can be full of the virus, and it can contaminate ponds and lakes.

In 1996 a new form of the H5N1 bird flu virus was discovered in geese in Guangdong, China. This virus has since become endemic in bird populations in six countries and has shown up in seventy-nine others. Occasionally, it has crossed over from birds to humans. This jump is uncommon, typically only affecting those who work closely with poultry. It's also been found in other animals such as tigers and civets.

Managing bird flu in wild birds is an incredibly challenging, perhaps impossible, endeavor. Curbing the spread of bird flu in domesticated birds such as ducks and chickens should be feasible. For example, in early 2022, a major avian flu outbreak struck the United States, prompting farmers to cull over 22.8 million birds across twenty-four states in an attempt to halt the spread of the virus.

Although birds are the main carriers, the WHO monitors avian flu outbreaks in mammals because infection of mammals by avian influenza viruses heightens the risk of viral adaptation. Such adaptations could then help the transmission between mammalian hosts, including humans. For example, in 2022 researchers found that the H5N1 avian flu virus discovered in geese in Guangdong had spilled over into the sea lion population in Peru and Chile and into elephant seals in Argentina. The virus underwent fifteen mutations, and now it can spread between the marine mammals themselves. The same fifteen mutations were also present in a Chilean man who was diagnosed with a case of avian flu in 2023.

As of 2025 the H5N1 virus has been found in US cows and their milk and in poultry including chickens, ducks, and geese. By early February sixty-seven people were confirmed to have contracted the virus, but it had not mutated to spread from person to person. Health officials continued to monitor the virus for potential developments.

THE ROLE OF GLOBAL MOBILITY IN THE SPREAD OF DISEASES

Many factors were responsible for the 1918 flu, including the increased movement of people and animals due to improvements in transport and the international deployment of troops. Travel was also crucial in the spread of the plague, and it will remain a contributing factor in the spread of many infectious diseases discussed in this book, as well as future infectious diseases. This is because as the global population continues to grow, travel increases, and the demand for access to foreign goods intensifies. The connection among modern societies leads to the rapid movement of pathogens across borders, increasing the risk of global outbreaks.

CHAPTER 3

DENGUE FEVER AND GLOBAL URBANIZATION

URBANIZATION AND INFECTIOUS DISEASES

The high concentration of people in urban areas, coupled with efficient transportation systems linking megacities worldwide, significantly increases the risk of cities to epidemic outbreaks and makes them centers of local disease transmission. As we saw in the previous chapter, pathogens can hitch a ride with international travelers and freight on both ships and planes, spreading disease from country to country. Once the pathogens arrive in a new country, local transmission is necessary for the disease outbreak to continue. This might be good news except for another key factor: Most airports and ports are within or nearby big cities that are responsible for accepting and further distributing the freight and associated germs.

For the first time in history, more people live in towns and cities (urban environments) than on farms and in the country (rural areas). Urbanization has predominantly occurred during the last two centuries. In 1800 fewer than 10 percent of the global population lived in urban areas. By 1960, 33 percent of people had moved into urban areas. And by 2000, 47 percent were living in cities and towns. As of 2024, it was over 55 percent. Although the definition of what constitutes "urban" varies around the world (for example, being defined by population size, density, infrastructure, employment nature, or predefined city boundaries), the overall trends are undeniable. People living in urban areas tend to have higher incomes than those in the country. And high-income countries have a larger urban population than low-income countries, which are mostly rural. Worldwide, the percentage of the population living in urban areas in Asia and Africa is currently the lowest, but it is expected to increase rapidly. People are moving into cities because urban areas provide better access to electricity, sanitation, clean water, and employment and have lower child malnutrition rates.

But the urban fabric is woven unevenly, creating barriers that prevent specific neighborhoods and demographic groups from accessing these urban advantages. Wealthier districts often benefit from better infrastructure, health care, educational opportunities, and job prospects, while economically disadvantaged neighborhoods are left behind. These areas may lack investment in basic amenities such as clean water, reliable transportation, and adequate sanitation, creating a stark divide between well-off and marginalized communities. Consequently, income inequality is greater in cities than in rural areas, where the social and economic landscape tends to be more uniform. In cities, this inequality not only manifests in economic disparities but also affects residents' quality of life, health outcomes, and life expectancy, reinforcing cycles of poverty that can persist for generations.

The rapid influx of people into cities often outpaces the development of adequate infrastructure, leading to overcrowding and the formation of shantytowns, or areas often on the outskirts of town where many people build and live in improvised housing. Worldwide, more than one-quarter of urban dwellers reside in informal settlements where the inhabitants lack basic human necessities, including reliable access to clean water, proper sanitation facilities, adequate living space, and structurally sound dwellings. In the cramped quarters of such

POPULATION DENSITY, 2024

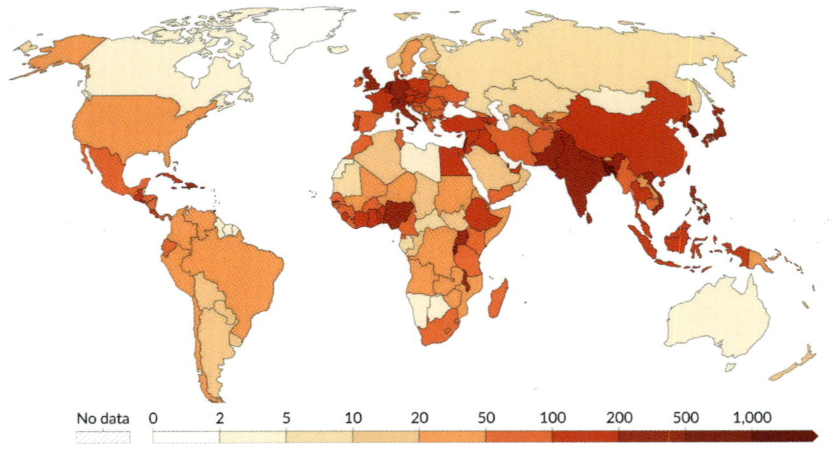

A map of world population density. The darker the shade, the more densely populated a country is per square kilometer.

settlements, diseases carried by insects and rodents flourish, posing significant health risks to residents. Some diseases such as cholera, a waterborne diarrheal disease, and tuberculosis are significantly more common in informal settlements than in other, wealthier parts of cities.

While severe disease is more common in densely packed neighborhoods such as informal settlements, the high population density across urban areas poses health risks citywide. Urban areas house more than 55 percent of the world's population yet occupy only 2 percent of global land. The close contact between people in urban areas and their high population density creates potential hot spots for the rapid spread of infectious diseases. These are the reasons why:

- The numerous and close interactions between people in densely populated towns and cities helps to transmit pathogens from person to person, accelerating the spread of infectious diseases.

- The environmental changes associated with rapid and often unregulated urban expansion create new frontiers where human and animal habitats overlap, escalating the potential for spillover. For instance, extensive deforestation driven by urban sprawl brings humans into more frequent contact with bats and primates, which could harbor viruses that can transition from animal to human. We'll discuss spillover in more detail in chapter 5.
- Certain pathogens and vectors are better suited to thrive in these densely populated urban environments. This boosts the acceleration of new diseases and the spread of old ones.

Dengue fever is a prime example of a disease linked to urbanization. As cities grow, they often lack the infrastructure needed to manage rapid population increases, leading to crowded living conditions and insufficient waste management. These environments create ideal breeding grounds for the mosquito species responsible for spreading dengue, as stagnant water from poorly maintained drains, discarded containers, and unregulated water storage becomes abundant.

HISTORY OF DENGUE FEVER

The earliest known accounts of symptoms resembling dengue fever trace back to a Chinese medical text from around 400 CE. These symptoms included fever, intestinal and oral bleeding, pain in the eyeballs, and rashes. Throughout history, there have been several accounts of dengue fever outbreaks. One outbreak was in Philadelphia in 1780, where dengue fever was first called *breakbone fever*. This name is still associated with the disease due to the intense joint pain that dengue fever causes. The name *dengue fever* most likely came from an 1801 epidemic in Madrid, where sore patients' fastidious and careful gait was responsible for the name—*dengue* in Spanish means "fastidiousness."

In 1922 a dengue fever outbreak spread through the Southeastern United States, infecting over five hundred thousand victims. This

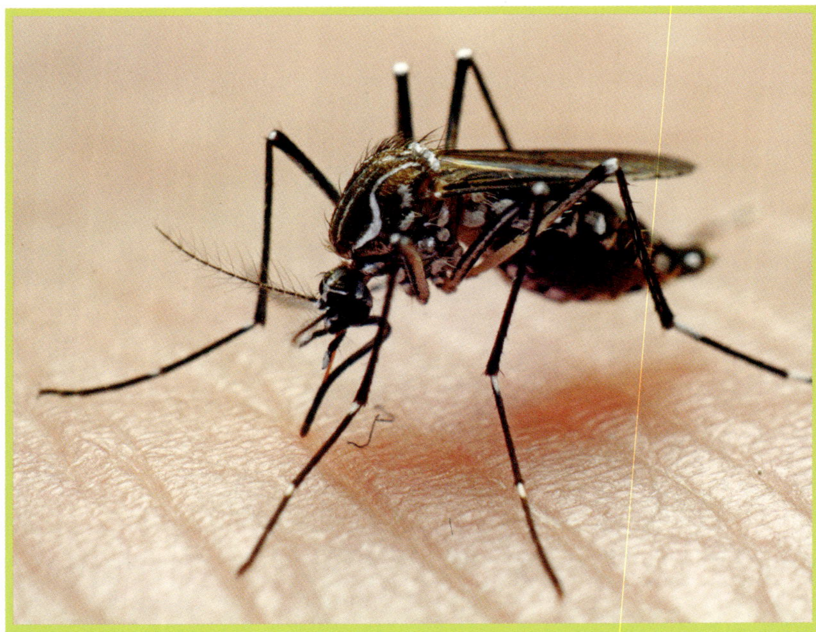

Mosquitoes are the main vectors of the dengue virus.

largest dengue fever outbreak in the United States led to a major ditching and drainage program to control malaria and *Aedes* mosquitoes, which spread dengue. This program was successful, and it limited future dengue fever outbreaks. In 1944 the war on dengue fever got a new weapon: aerial spraying of DDT, an effective pesticide against mosquitoes. Within three years, the dengue mosquito was eliminated in the United States, and for the next fifty years, the only dengue fever cases in the United States were returning tourists who had been bitten abroad. But DDT harmed the environment, especially bird populations, so it was banned in the United States in 1972, and the dengue mosquito has slowly made its way back into the country.

The Centers for Disease Control and Prevention (CDC) describe the primary symptoms of dengue fever as high fever; intense headache; severe eye pain; joint, muscle, and bone pain; rashes; and mild bleeding. Younger children and those experiencing their first infection tend to have less severe symptoms than older children, teenagers, and adults.

Early reports of more severe forms of the disease, called dengue hemorrhagic fever and dengue shock syndrome, were recorded in Australia in 1897 and Greece in 1928. Dengue hemorrhagic fever includes a fever lasting two to seven days with symptoms similar to dengue fever. As the fever subsides, more severe symptoms can develop, such as persistent vomiting, severe abdominal pain, respiratory difficulties, a low platelet count, and bleeding tendencies, which may manifest as easy bruising, nose and gum bleeding, or even internal hemorrhaging. This period, which lasts twenty-four to forty-eight hours, is critical, as the capillaries may become overly permeable (they hemorrhage), potentially leading to circulatory system collapse. This then causes massive hemorrhaging from the eyes, nose, mouth, and vagina, as well as multiple organ and respiratory failure. This is called dengue shock syndrome, and it can be fatal if it is not promptly treated.

Between 1 and 5 percent of dengue fever patients die if they get no medical treatment. But with intravenous hydration, those numbers drop close to zero. Dengue shock syndrome has a mortality rate of 10 to 20 percent. Fortunately, the rate drops to 1 percent with the correct medical treatment.

THE DENGUE VIRUS

In 1907 US army doctors P. M. Ashburn and Charles F. Craig discovered that a tiny, round virus causes dengue fever. At the time, the only other disease known to be caused by a virus was yellow fever. Because the dengue virus was so closely related to the yellow fever virus, it was classified into the same viral genus, the *Orthoflavivirus* genus. The genus name comes from the Latin word for "yellow" (flavus) because the genus's viruses are all similar to the yellow fever virus. Other well-known viruses in this genus include Zika, Japanese encephalitis, and West Nile encephalitis.

The dengue viruses are simple and small, allowing them to avoid immediate detection by the human immune system. They do not need a complex life cycle to survive and can be undetected in the human bloodstream for two to seven days. During this time, they can infect other *Aedes* mosquitoes that bite the infected individual.

The four types of dengue viruses are DENV-1, DENV-2, DENV-3, and DENV-4. These are serotypes—distinct variations of a bacteria or virus—of the dengue virus. They all originated from a shared ancestral virus found in nonhuman primates before each of the four serotypes separately transitioned from animal hosts to humans.

The serotypes can impact the severity of dengue fever. Patients never get dengue hemorrhagic or dengue shock fever on their first round of dengue fever. These forms of dengue have only been observed in patients who had dengue fever in the past and had a second bout caused by a different dengue virus serotype than the one that caused the first bout. The longer the time between the two infections with different serotypes, the more severe the symptoms of the dengue hemorrhagic and dengue shock fever tend to be.

A dengue vaccine is available in some countries. It protects against dengue hemorrhagic fever and dengue shock syndrome and is given only to patients who have had a confirmed case of dengue fever in the past.

THE DISEASE LIFE CYCLE OF THE DENGUE VIRUS

Scientists have sequenced dengue viruses' genetic material (RNA). While the four dengue virus serotypes only share about 65 percent of their genetic material, they cause virtually identical symptoms. The relatively uncomplicated dengue viruses, containing RNA that codes for just 10 of its own proteins, can alter the production of 147 distinct proteins in the dengue mosquito. These modifications increase the mosquito's appetite for human blood, make its saliva more hospitable for the virus, and alter the protein composition in the mosquito's antennae, which heightens its sensitivity to smells, thus improving the mosquito's efficiency in locating a host.

Dengue viruses reside within an infected mosquito's gut lining. About eight to ten days after the mosquito has been infected, it can transmit the virus to humans through its bite. The mosquito remains physically healthy and seemingly unaffected by the virus, carries it for life, and can pass it on to its offspring via its eggs. Dengue mosquitoes have a lifespan averaging three weeks, and they must be at least two weeks old before they are capable of transmitting dengue viruses.

When an infected mosquito bites a person, the virus is transferred into the human bloodstream. It replicates within cells in the immune system and the lymph nodes before returning to the bloodstream and spreading to other tissues. Once back in the bloodstream, the virus can trigger an immune response, leading to symptoms such as fever, rash, and muscle pain.

DENGUE MOSQUITOES

Aedes aegypti mosquitoes are the primary dengue vectors. *Aedes* mosquitoes prefer to feed on human blood. But they also target other warm-blooded animals when they can't find human victims. Although *Aedes aegypti* are native to Africa, thanks to urbanization, international travel, and global trade, they are now widespread in tropical and subtropical regions all over the world and thrive in temperatures between 59°F and 95°F (15°C and 35°C). These stealthy bloodsuckers don't keep you up at night. They are smaller than most other mosquito species, more active during the day than at night, and less noisy than the mosquitoes typically found in North America. *Aedes* are ankle biters, and their most active feeding hours are in the early morning and later in the afternoon.

Aedes albopictus mosquitoes, also known as Asian tiger mosquitoes, can carry the dengue virus, but not as efficiently as *Aedes aegypti*. *Aedes aegypti* and *Aedes albopictus* are almost identical. A magnifying glass is needed to differentiate between the two. Other mosquito species can carry the dengue virus, but only *Aedes aegypti* and *Aedes albopictus* can pass the dengue virus onto future mosquito generations and are largely responsible for the spread of the disease.

Like all other mosquito species, only pregnant female *Aedes* mosquitoes bite people. Their blood meals supply the pregnant mosquitoes with the nutrients they need to produce healthy eggs. When a female mosquito feeds, her abdomen expands, and she can hold up to three times her body weight in blood. Male mosquitoes do not have the correct mouthparts for piercing human skin and sucking blood. They feed on plant nectar instead.

Aedes mosquitoes fly no more than 1,312 feet (400 m) total in their lives. Due to this limited flight range, *Aedes* need areas with high population density to get enough blood meals. So this urban-dwelling mosquito species is more common in cities than in forested areas. They have been domesticated and have adapted to living in close quarters with humans in cities and towns. *Aedes* mosquitoes lay their eggs in containers such as metal drums, earthen jars, and other discarded items capable of holding rainwater, including bottle tops and unused tires. They don't need ponds and lakes to breed. They tend to live inside homes, hiding in dimly lit areas such as closets and cabinets, from where the silent bloodsuckers can go and bite up to twenty individuals in a single day without being noticed.

Controlling these mosquitoes is challenging because they can breed in just a few drops of water and prefer environments close to human dwellings, where using pesticide sprays might pose human health risks. Also, mosquito nets, which typically hang over someone's bed to keep them from being bitten at night, are not effective at controlling *Aedes* mosquitoes because they bite during the day when victims are not in bed.

DENGUE FEVER IN THE FUTURE

An estimated one hundred million to four hundred million people get dengue every year. Between 50 and 90 percent of dengue

AEDES AEGYPTI, YELLOW FEVER, AND THE PANAMA CANAL

Aedes mosquitoes are a primary vector for yellow fever, which halted progress on the Panama Canal in the 1880s when the French first attempted to build it. The disease had a high mortality rate and struck fear among the workers on the canal. With symptoms including fever, jaundice, and internal bleeding, yellow fever was both deadly and terrifying. Outbreaks would cause widespread panic, leading to a high turnover of workers and stalling progress on construction. Understanding and controlling yellow fever became essential for the completion of the canal.

Panama was not the first place William Crawford Gorgas helped halt disease outbreaks. Between 1900 and 1902, he also culled typhoid and yellow fever outbreaks in Havana, Cuba.

The proximity of *Aedes aegypti* to human populations made it challenging to control, especially in densely populated areas with poor sanitation. It was essential to limit mosquito breeding sites and reduce contact between mosquitoes and humans. When the United States assumed control of the Panama Canal project, the high prevalence of mosquito-borne diseases threatened its completion. Recognizing this, Colonel William Crawford Gorgas, the chief sanitary officer, implemented a groundbreaking mosquito control program in 1905. His team drained standing water, killed mosquito larvae with chemicals, and installed screens on windows to prevent mosquitoes from entering homes. They also fumigated (disinfected with chemical fumes) houses where cases had developed and quarantined yellow fever patients in screened quarters.

Through aggressive inspection and policing of breeding sites, yellow fever was eradicated from the Canal Zone by 1906, enabling the project to continue. This public health success allowed for the completion of the Panama Canal and became a milestone in environmental and disease control efforts, paving the way for advancements in tropical medicine.

cases are mild and sometimes even asymptomatic, so they go unreported. It is estimated that only 10 percent of dengue cases are recorded. Still, in 2023, over five million people sought medical attention for dengue fever, and there were more than five thousand dengue-associated deaths.

Dengue fever is currently twenty times more common than the flu. But it hasn't always been this way. Between 1947 and 1965, *Aedes* eradication programs were effective in preventing the spread of yellow fever, which is also spread by the *Aedes* mosquito. But there has been a Dengue resurgence, with thirty times more infections in 2010 than in 1960. The convergence of multiple factors—including the discontinued use of DDT, the development of an effective vaccine for yellow fever, rapid population growth, urban expansion, and global warming—has led to the significant global return of *Aedes aegypti* and, consequently, dengue fever. As a result, dengue has become one of the most rapidly spreading infectious diseases globally, posing a major threat to public health in both endemic and newly affected tropical regions. It is regularly found in over one hundred countries (endemic), and the most significant increases have been in the Caribbean and Central America.

To address the growing burden of dengue, innovative approaches are needed that consider not only biological factors but also the broader social, economic, and environmental influences shaping disease transmission. Only through a response that acknowledges the complexities of urbanization and climate change expanding warm regions that suit the *Aedes* mosquito can we hope to curb the spread of dengue and mitigate its impact on vulnerable populations worldwide.

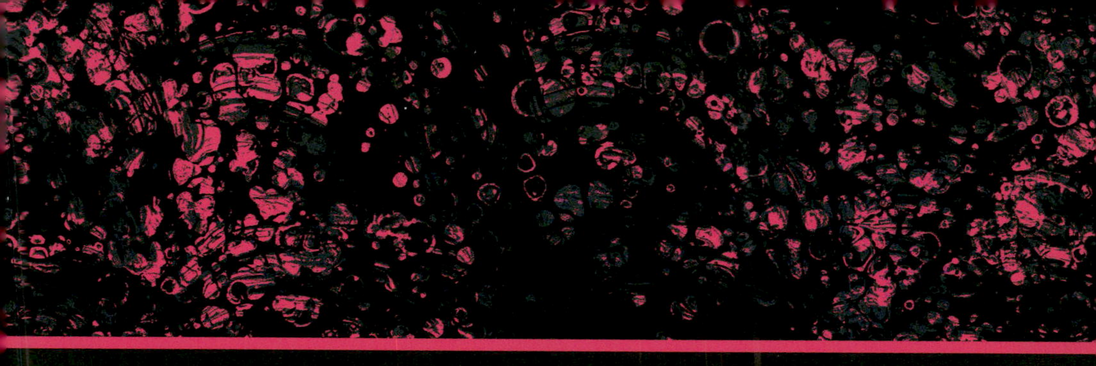

CHAPTER 4

MALARIA AND CLIMATE CHANGE

CLIMATE CHANGE

The greenhouse effect was first recognized in 1827 when the French mathematician Joseph Fourier proposed that some atmospheric gases trap heat on Earth like a pane of glass in a greenhouse traps warmth. He has since been proved right. Without greenhouse gases such as carbon dioxide and methane trapping the infrared radiation from Earth and the sun, preventing it from leaving the atmosphere, Earth's average temperature would be –0.4°F (–18°C). All water would be frozen, and there would be no life as we know it. The greenhouse effect warms Earth to a hospitable average temperature of 59°F (15°C), supporting the diverse life-forms seen on Earth.

While the greenhouse effect is a natural phenomenon, climate change is driven by human activities that significantly increase greenhouse gas levels in the atmosphere. These elevated greenhouse gas concentrations have led to a rise in average global temperatures, surpassing 59°F (15°C) and contributing to widespread environmental impacts. The primary sources of these gas emissions are burning fossil fuels, industrial processes such as cement production, deforestation, and agricultural practices, especially cow, pig, and rice production.

The National Aeronautics and Space Administration (NASA) does a monthly analysis of global temperatures obtained from sixty-three hundred meteorological stations around the world. These include ship- and buoy-based instruments measuring sea surface temperatures, and Antarctic research stations. According to NASA, 2023 was the warmest year since global records began in 1850, with temperatures 2.12°F (1.18°C) above the national average—until 2024 broke that record with even higher temperatures. And 16 of the 17 warmest years in the 136 years that NASA has recorded temperatures have occurred since 2001. (The one exception was 1998.)

CLIMATE CHANGE AND DISEASE

Climate change is responsible for long-term changes in temperature and weather patterns, which cause increased sea levels, the retreat of glaciers, the melting of polar ice, and changes in precipitation patterns. Scientists anticipate that climate change will also be responsible for causing around 250,000 additional deaths annually due to associated undernutrition, malaria, waterborne diseases, and heat stress. An analysis of 830 published peer-reviewed articles related to diseases affected by climatic conditions revealed that 58 percent of infectious diseases (218 out of 375) have at some point been aggravated by climatic hazards, and 16 percent were less severe. By 2030 climate change's estimated annual financial impact on health will range from $2 billion to $4 billion. Regions with fragile health-care systems are expected to struggle the most in preparing for and dealing with these challenges.

TEMPERATURE RISE EFFECTS

Worldwide, thousands of people die from heat-related causes each year, most of them during intense heat waves. As the number of heat waves increases due to climate change, these deaths will increase too. Extreme heat affects the heart (blood vessels dilate and blood pressure drops, which can cause heart attacks), brain (headaches and disrupted sleep), lungs (aggravates respiratory conditions), and kidneys (dehydration can lead to chronic kidney disease). Increasing temperatures also decrease our cognitive abilities. For instance, a 2024 study showed that students who took a math test at temperatures above 90°F (32°C) scored roughly the same as students who had a quarter of a year fewer math classes and took the test at 72°F to 75°F (22°C to 24°C).

In this book, we are more concerned with the link between climate change and diseases.

PERMAFROST AND METHUSELAH PATHOGENS

The Arctic is warming four times faster than the rest of the world. Two-thirds of the Arctic Sea ice has disappeared since 1958, and scientists project that two-thirds of the Arctic's near-surface permafrost could be gone by 2100. Permafrost is a permanently frozen layer of soil, gravel, and sand, usually bound together by ice, that remains frozen for two or more consecutive years. Some of it has been frozen for tens or even hundreds of thousands of years. It covers a fifth of the Northern Hemisphere.

Permafrost is dark and cold and lacks oxygen, perfect for preserving human bodies and the pathogens that killed them. As permafrost thaws due to climate change, bacteria and viruses hidden underground for tens of thousands of years are being uncovered. Scientists have revived a thirty-thousand-year-old virus that infects amoebas and discovered microbes more than four hundred thousand years old. These old pathogens are known as Methuselah microbes and zombie viruses. Thanks to climate change, we are vulnerable to defrosted diseases from the distant past.

Getting infected by a Methuselah pathogen is not a hypothetical scenario. Between June and August 2016, the average air temperature in northern Siberia was higher than any recorded in the previous thirty years. Permafrost melted and reindeer carcasses defrosted. Some of those reindeer had died from an anthrax outbreak that occurred seventy-five years ago. The anthrax spores entered the soil, water and, eventually, the food supply. They infected 2,650 reindeer (6.46 percent of the susceptible population), and 2,350 of these infected reindeer died. Some anthrax spillover occurred, and a hundred people in Siberia were hospitalized, including a boy who died from the disease.

WATERBORNE DISEASES

Water has a high heat capacity. That means it is very good at absorbing heat, and that is why 90 percent of global warming occurs in the ocean. The average surface temperature of the world's oceans has been increasing at an average rate of 0.14°F (0.08°C) per decade from 1901 through 2020, and the global sea surface temperature in 2023 was significantly higher than any measured year before that (see chart below).

Vibrio are bacteria that inhabit surface waters throughout the world. They are responsible for several severe infections in humans and animals. Human *Vibrio* illnesses are increasing worldwide. They

AVERAGE GLOBAL SEA SURFACE TEMPERATURE, 1880–2023

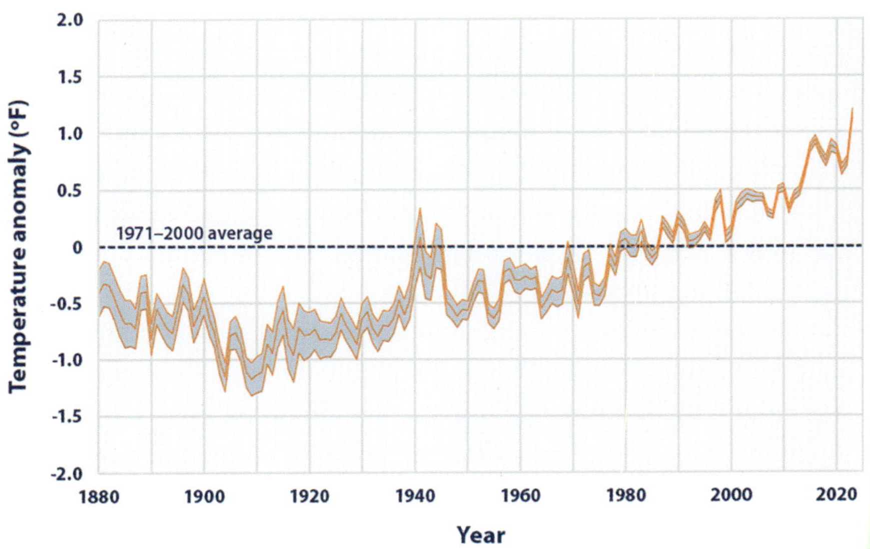

include fatal diarrheal diseases such as cholera, gastroenteritis, wound infections, and septicemia. *Vibrio* infections can occur when someone ingests raw or undercooked seafood or is exposed to seawater.

Partly due to global warming and the fact that *Vibrio* thrive in waters warmer than 59°F (15°C), infections have increased between the early 2000s and 2024 and have spread toward the poles into areas not usually associated with these bacteria. In 2014 an unusual heat wave crept to within 99 miles (160 km) of the Arctic Circle, warming the ocean's surface waters. The waters became breeding grounds for *Vibrio* bacteria, causing unprecedented outbreaks of *Vibrio*-related disease, especially cholera, in coastal Finland and Sweden.

Warming waters are also responsible for harmful algal blooms, found in both freshwater and saltwater environments. These blooms release toxins that pose health risks to humans and animals through contaminated seafood, especially shellfish, and water.

EXPANDING VECTOR HABITATS

As global temperatures rise, some fungi that cause diseases have begun to inhabit regions that were once too cold for their survival. Fungi are a diverse group of organisms that include mushrooms, molds, and yeast. They can be found almost everywhere—in water, soil, and air; inside homes; and even on and within the human body. While most fungal infections don't pose a severe health threat and aren't life-threatening, some do cause diseases.

As the difference between the average outdoor temperature and the human body temperature narrows due to global warming, new fungal diseases such as valley fever may emerge because the fungi will become more adapted to surviving in humans with a similar internal body temperature as their environment. Valley fever, or coccidioidomycosis, is a fungal infection caused by inhaling microscopic fungal spores in the air. The spores can lead to infections in some people who inhale them. Symptoms include coughing, high temperature, weariness, breathlessness, headaches, and pain in muscles or joints. Valley fever

LYME DISEASE: A CLIMATE CHANGE INDICATOR

The Environmental Protection Agency (EPA) has more than fifty indicators that illustrate the causes and effects of climate change. The indicators are designed to help us understand observed long-term climate change trends. Lyme disease is one of the EPA's climate change indicators.

Since 1991 the rate of Lyme disease cases has nearly doubled from 3.74 cases per 100,000 individuals in 1991 to 7.21 cases per 100,000 individuals in 2018. This increase has been attributed to climate change, alterations in land use patterns, and increased interactions between people and wildlife.

Lyme disease is the most common vector-borne disease in the United States. This bacterial infection can result in symptoms such as fever, exhaustion, joint pain, a characteristic skin rash, and neurological complications. At least twenty thousand to thirty thousand cases of Lyme disease are reported annually. The bite from an infected deer tick species spreads Lyme disease. While deer are common hosts for these ticks, they do not carry the Lyme disease bacteria themselves. Instead, the ticks acquire the bacteria from other hosts such as white-footed mice.

The life cycle and abundance of deer ticks depend on temperature. Deer ticks thrive when temperatures exceed 45°F (7.2°C) and the humidity levels are at least 85 percent. They prefer the shorter, warmer winters and prolonged, warmer summers associated with climate change. Their habitat has expanded since warmer average temperatures mean they can survive in areas previously too hot or cold.

TRANSMISSION OF BACTERIA THAT CAUSE LYME DISEASE

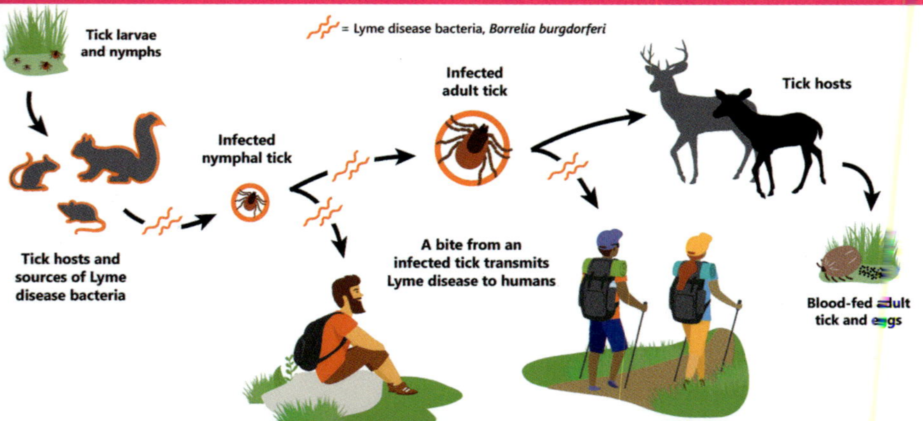

is frequently misdiagnosed, and if not treated correctly, it can cause serious and sometimes fatal infections. It is endemic to the hot, arid soils in the Southwestern United States and parts of Mexico. But because of climate change, its range has expanded into the Pacific Northwest, where it was previously unknown.

Milder winters, fewer frost days, and warmer summers not only will allow fungi to spread into new geographical areas and cross into humans, but they will enable vectors such as mosquitoes and ticks to expand their habitats and spread infectious diseases to new parts of the world. From 2004 to 2018, mosquito-, tick-, and flea-borne diseases more than doubled in the United States, surpassing 760,000 total cases, and nine new pathogens carried by these vectors appeared in the country. Diseases transmitted by ticks, including Lyme disease, anaplasmosis, ehrlichiosis, and spotted fever, have expanded their range. Warmer and longer summers also mean that ticks emerge and start biting earlier in the season and that the animals that carry the ticks, such as rodents, deer, and raccoons, are venturing into new territories.

Climate change allows some animals to expand their habitat, while other species are forced to move to entirely new territories as theirs become inhospitable to them. These shifts in animal distribution heighten the likelihood of new encounters between humans and animals and between animal species whose habitats have never overlapped before, thereby raising the risk of transmission of new zoonotic diseases. For instance, the temperatures in Arctic regions are increasing at more than four times the global average rate. In Alaska this rapid warming results in a rise in vole populations, heightening the risk of spreading animal-carried diseases such as borealpox (formerly Alaskapox) to human populations.

MORE ON MOSQUITOES

There are over thirty-five hundred species of mosquitoes worldwide. They live on every continent except Antarctica. In the United States, there are over two hundred types of mosquitoes, and twelve of these types are known to spread diseases. The mosquito species have different temperature preferences for spreading diseases. For instance, malaria transmission is most prevalent at temperatures around 78°F (25°C), whereas Zika virus transmission peaks at temperatures close to 84°F (29°C). Extended and warmer summers also afford mosquitoes greater opportunities for breeding and transmitting diseases. The 2012 weather conditions, characterized by a mild winter, an early spring, and a scorching summer, paved the way for a significant West Nile virus outbreak in the United States, resulting in over fifty-six hundred cases and 286 deaths.

The CDC calls mosquitoes the "world's deadliest animal." Although they weigh just 0.000088 ounces (2.5 mg), they are the vectors for some of the world's deadliest diseases, including malaria, dengue, West Nile, yellow fever, Zika, chikungunya, and lymphatic filariasis. Mosquitoes cause more than seven hundred thousand deaths each year.

Malaria is the deadliest mosquito-borne disease. Nearly 3.2 billion people live in areas habitable to malaria mosquitoes.

Because all mosquito species have short life cycles and are dependent on their environmental conditions, they are very sensitive to climate change. Warmer global temperatures and altered rainfall patterns create more hospitable conditions for mosquitoes that transmit malaria. These changes expand the geographical range where mosquitoes can live and breed, increasing the incidence and reach of malaria. Let's look at this disease more closely.

MALARIA IN HISTORY

From six-thousand-year-old Mesopotamian tablets to the ancient texts of the Hindi surgeon Dhanvantari in 800 BCE to the writings of Homer, Plato, and Shakespeare, malaria has been described as a source of agony, suffering, and death. The ancient Chinese knew that malaria was associated with an enlarged spleen, but no one realized that mosquitoes were responsible for the disease.

PARASITES

Parasites live inside or on an organism that is called the host. Parasites obtain their food from their hosts, but they usually do not cause their host's death. But they can transmit diseases to their hosts that may be fatal. There are many types of parasites: single-celled protozoans that cause diseases such as malaria, sleeping sickness, and amoebic dysentery; various animals such as hookworms, lice, mosquitoes, and vampire bats; fungi such as the honey fungus; and parasitic plants such as mistletoe, dodder, and broomrapes.

In Italy, malaria was rampant during the Roman Empire, and the Romans assumed that it was the foul smells from the surrounding wetlands and marshes that were responsible for the headaches, high fevers, bone-shaking chills, and pains associated with malaria. Like the medieval Europeans and the plague, the Romans thought the miasma, or bad air, was responsible for all diseases including malaria. "Bad air" is *mala aria* in Latin, so they called the disease malaria. The first recorded use of the word *malaria* in the English language was in a 1740 letter from Horace Walpole, describing malaria's deadly presence in Rome each summer.

MALARIA PARASITES

In 1880, while stationed at a military hospital in Algeria, French army physician Charles Laveran became the first doctor to detect malaria parasites in the red blood cells of patients with the disease. Later, in Rome, he treated Italian soldiers suffering from malaria and found the same parasites in the blood of 148 out of 200 patient samples. He also discovered that the parasites vanished from the bloodstream when the patients were treated with quinine, a known antimalarial medication (see more on page 65).

The malaria parasites belong to the genus *Plasmodia*. They spend their lives going back and forth between humans and mosquitoes. They cannot be transmitted from person to person without passing through a mosquito. There are 156 species of *Plasmodia*. The two most common malaria parasites that infect humans are *Plasmodium falciparum* and *Plasmodium vivax*. *P. falciparum* is the more common and deadlier form of the two parasites. It can live only in tropical mosquitoes and mainly is found in Africa. But climate change and the associated rise in global temperature are increasing the areas vulnerable to malaria. *P. falciparum* can infect up to 80 percent of the victim's blood, forty times more than *P. vivax*. *P. vivax* makes its home in Asian and Latin American mosquitoes. Although it has a lower mortality than *P. falciparum*, it can hide in the human liver, where it is difficult to treat, so it often defies treatment and escapes detection.

But where did this parasite come from, and how did it get into humans?

To answer this question, in 2010 Beatrice Hahn from the Department of Medicine at the University of Alabama and her coworkers collected the feces from three thousand wild apes in central Africa and searched through all the poop to see if any of it contained DNA similar to the DNA of *P. falciparum*. The poop from eastern gorillas and bonobos contained no *Plasmodia* DNA. Meanwhile, half the chimpanzee feces and a third of all western gorilla feces contained malarial DNA. By comparing the *Plasmodia* DNA of the chimpanzee and the western gorilla to that of *P. falciparum*, which causes malaria in humans, Hahn's team was able to show that *P. falciparum* was a gorilla parasite before it made the transition to humans.

MALARIA-CARRYING MOSQUITOES

Fifteen years after Laveran discovered *Plasmodia*, researchers showed that mosquitoes transmitted the malaria parasites to humans. But it was not just any mosquitoes—a very specific type, the *Anopheles* mosquito, carried *Plasmodia*. Of the thirty-two hundred mosquito species, only about seventy, all from the *Anopheles* genus, are *Plasmodia* vectors. *P. falciparum* is only in female *Anopheles*. As with dengue fever, only female mosquitoes transmit malaria, as they are the ones that have blood meals. These meals are a necessary part of the parasite's life cycle and its spread to humans.

Sub-Saharan Africa faces the most severe impacts from mosquito-borne disease, as it has the right climatic conditions for the deadliest malaria parasite, *P. falciparum*, and the most efficient vector, *Anopheles gambiae*. This mosquito is aggressive, doesn't hibernate at low temperatures as some other species do, and exclusively feeds on human blood, making it an ideal transmitter of malaria parasites.

Anopheles stephensi are not as aggressive as *Anopheles gambiae* mosquitoes, but they are of concern to mosquito researchers because, like the dengue mosquitoes (*Aedes aegypti*), they are urban-dwelling mosquitoes that do well in hot, dry habitats. As climate change progresses, they are carrying malaria to new populations that have not been exposed to malaria and have no immunity to *P. falciparum*.

THE LIFE CYCLE OF THE MALARIA PARASITE

Female *Anopheles gambiae* mosquitoes bite because they need the hemoglobin in blood to nourish the eggs they are about to lay. Malaria parasites also need hemoglobin to provide them with the amino acids necessary for their survival and reproduction. Hemoglobin is in our red blood cells, where it is responsible for blood's deep red color and for transporting oxygen from our lungs to cells all over the body.

Plasmodia live in the salivary glands of *Anopheles* mosquitoes for part of their lives. When infected mosquitoes bite their victims, they inject some saliva into the puncture wound to prevent the blood from coagulating (clotting) and blocking the bite. In each bite, between ten and one hundred *Plasmodia* make the transition from the mosquito salivary glands to the human host. To evade the human immune system, which sends white blood cells to eliminate the invading *Plasmodia*, the malaria parasites make their way to the liver. Immune security at the liver is minimal because the liver is a waste treatment organ where our bodies send undesirable molecules for processing

THE LIFE CYCLE OF MALARIA PARASITES

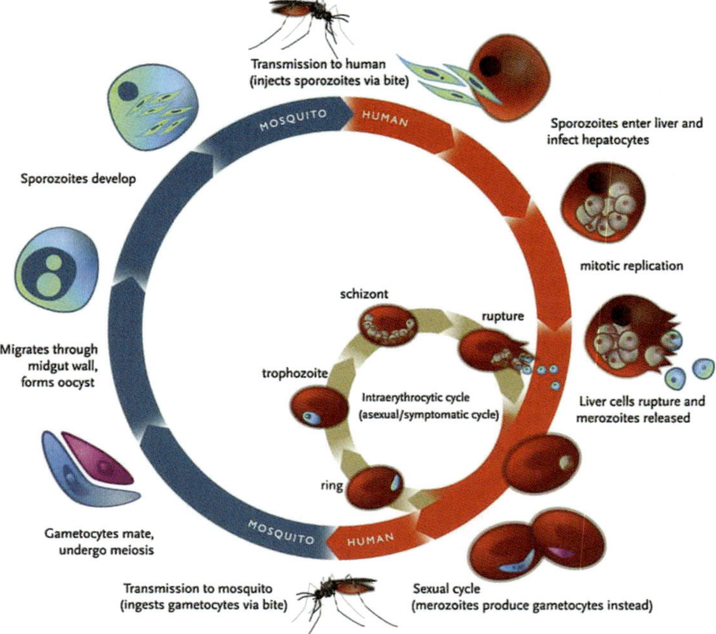

P. falciparum undergoes ten morphological transitions in its life cycle. It needs all ten forms to evade the very different molecular defense mechanisms that the mosquito and human immune systems throw at it. The malaria parasite lives in five different tissues, propagates asexually in three of them, and reproduces sexually at each transfer between hosts.

before they are excreted via feces. Most *Plasmodia* get caught before they reach the liver. The surviving *Plasmodia* spend about three to five days in the relative safety of the organ, where they undergo an asexual reproductive cycle to form about fifty thousand new parasites called merozoites. The merozoites enter dying liver cells to disguise themselves from the immune system as they reenter the bloodstream and start their quest for hemoglobin.

Some merozoites manage to invade the red blood cells that house hemoglobin. In the red blood cells, they digest the hemoglobin and asexually multiply until the red blood cells are full of malaria parasites.

Since all the merozoites leave the liver simultaneously, the infected red blood cells reach capacity at the same time. About forty-eight to seventy-two hours after the malaria parasites leave the liver, the red blood cells burst, spewing the merozoites and their waste into the blood. The host's immune system realizes it has been invaded and launches countermeasures, forcing the merozoites to invade new, healthy red blood cells, where they hide, multiply, and digest some more hemoglobin until the cells burst again.

With each cycle, more red blood cells are invaded, burst, and release more malaria parasites. Every time a new generation of parasites is released, along with its associated waste, the host experiences fevers, headaches, and nausea. If left untreated, the number of parasites increases by a factor of ten every two days. By the end of the infection, an infected individual can have close to a trillion *Plasmodium falciparum*. Then the symptoms can progress to severe fatigue,

USING PESTICIDES TO CONTROL MALARIA MOSQUITOES

More people have died from malaria than from any other disease in history. Malaria used to be common in southern parts of Europe and the United States, but thanks to the spraying of the insecticide DDT and the drainage of standing water, *Anopheles* mosquitoes were eliminated in these countries.

But reduced effectiveness and the danger to birds of prey led to the global banning of DDT, except in areas with high *Anopheles* and malaria concentrations. Traditional insecticides such as DDT are not good for the environment. They often are sprayed over large areas, are indiscriminate insecticides (they will kill mosquitoes but also bees and butterflies), and are toxic to noninsects such as birds. The harmful impacts of DDT have led to new methods of controlling malaria, including more focused ways of applying insecticides, such as insecticide-treated mosquito bed nets that act as a physical barrier to repel and kill mosquitoes, and the engineering of genetically modified *Anopheles* that are inhospitable to the malaria parasites.

confusion, seizures, and difficulty breathing. The spleen is responsible for clearing out red blood cell debris, but it can't handle the large number of burst red blood cells and can swell up to twenty times its standard size.

When the *Plasmodia* are ready to leave the human host, they change from small merozoites to larger gametocytes. Up to a trillion gametocytes cruise the human bloodstream in red blood cells, so that an *Anopheles* mosquito will ingest one of the red blood cells they have commandeered. Once in the mosquito, the gametocytes reproduce in the mosquito's gut and release a chemical that makes the mosquito less hungry, thereby protecting the parasites from being squashed by an irritated human during their host mosquito's blood meal. The cycle is completed when the gametocytes change form once again. This time, they become motile (capable of movement on their own) sporozoites before leaving the gut to swim up to the mosquito's salivary gland, where the cycle begins again. There can be up to twenty thousand sporozoites in the salivary glands of one mosquito, but the mosquitoes never eject more than one thousand per blood meal.

Once the parasites are in the mosquito's salivary glands, they restore the mosquito's appetite and decrease the amount of anticoagulants in the mosquito's saliva. Consequently, during a blood meal, the victim's blood clots up before the mosquito is full, causing her to bite more often. This is not in the mosquito's best interest since each bite jeopardizes her, but the malaria parasite gets another chance to infect a new host.

Pregnant female *Anopheles* mosquitoes track down their human blood meals by following traces of carbon dioxide and lactic acid released from the skin, sweat, and breath, and by following the scent of smelly feet. Mosquitoes have taste receptors not only on their tongue but also on their feet. So, as soon as they land on a potential host, they can taste it and assess whether the victim is worth biting.

Malaria parasites in humans seem to enhance their host's appeal to mosquitoes by causing them to emit an additional unique odor.

This scent increases the likelihood that mosquitoes will prefer to bite individuals infected with malaria over those not infected, thereby boosting the parasite's chances of being spread to new hosts.

ANTIMALARIAL DRUGS

There are two ways to combat malaria. One is to use insecticides, bed nets, and genetically modified mosquitoes to control the size of the *Anopheles* population and its ability to spread the malaria parasite to humans. The other is to attack the *Plasmodia* in their human hosts—to treat malaria medically.

In the fifteenth century, the Quechua people in Peru made a drink from the bark of cinchona trees to treat diarrhea and to prevent shivering, including the shivering from malarial fevers. Spanish Jesuit missionaries observed the Quechua's medicinal use of the cinchona bark, recorded it in their writings, and brought it back to Europe in 1636, where it became known as Jesuits' bark and was used to treat malaria. From the 1640s to 1820, apothecaries and early pharmacists prepared the antimalarial extract by drying cinchona bark, grinding it into a fine powder, and dissolving it in wine or another liquid to mask its taste.

In 1820 two French chemists, Pierre Pelletier and Joseph Caventou, isolated the active ingredient in the cinchona bark. The purified active ingredient, called quinine, was used as the standard treatment for malaria. It was the first use of a known chemical compound to treat an infectious disease. In 1861 an Australian alpaca farmer brought cinchona seeds from Peru to Java (an Indonesian island) and India. By 1900 two-thirds of the world's quinine production originated from Java, and by 1930 Dutch orchards in Java produced 22 million pounds (10 million kg) of quinine each year (97 percent of the world market at the time). But because malaria *Plasmodia* in many parts of the world have become resistant to quinine and because there are much better treatments for malaria, since 2006 the World Health Organization no longer recommends quinine as a primary treatment for malaria.

Tonic water was first developed as a way to consume quinine and therefore treat or prevent malaria. The main ingredients in tonic water remain carbonated water, a sweetener, and quinine. Quinine gives the drink its mildly bitter flavor.

Artemisinin-based combination therapies (ACTs) are the most effective antimalarial drugs. The WHO recommends them for *P. falciparum* infections, and people use them worldwide. It has been estimated that more than one hundred million malaria patients have been saved from hospitalization because they were treated with ACTs.

Artemisinin has a fascinating history. It was discovered during the Chinese Cultural Revolution (1966–1977), a time of criticism and persecution against scientists and scientific theories. In 1967 on the order of Chairman Mao, Chinese scientists started a secret initiative to find a cure for malaria that could help the North Vietnamese troops fighting in the Vietnam War. They were fighting in the mosquito-infested jungles of North Vietnam and had no access to quinine or any other effective treatment against the malaria parasite. Tens of thousands of North Vietnamese died from malaria. But fewer than fifty American soldiers died from malaria because they had access to quinine, which was effective against the malaria strain found in the Vietnamese jungles.

The malaria military research effort, Project 523, was launched on May 23, 1967, to find an alternative antimalarial drug to quinine. Named after its launch date, the project employed more than five hundred scientists from numerous research institutes. In January 1969 Professor Youyou Tu joined the program. She was tasked with searching through two thousand recipes of traditional Chinese herbal medicines for compounds with antimalarial properties. Her group found a plant called *Artemisia annua* (sweet wormwood tree), which appeared in many recipes. Extracts from more than one hundred *Artemisia annua* were tested on the rodent malaria parasites *Plasmodium berghei*. The results were OK, but not great, and inconsistent.

One day, Tu was reading a medical description from 340 CE written by a physician, Ge Hong, titled "Emergency Prescriptions Kept Up One's Sleeve." In it, Hong describes how to obtain "juice" from the *Artemisia* plant using cold water. Tu realized that she should try a room-temperature extraction to collect the juice from the plant, unlike most other Chinese herbal medicines, which are prepared by boiling. Perhaps the high temperatures used in the extraction were degrading the active ingredient in the *Artemisia* plant.

On October 9, 1971, using the leaves of the sweet wormwood plant and a room-temperature extraction, Tu obtained a sample that could inhibit rodent and monkey malaria with 100 percent efficiency. Subsequent tests on twenty-one people infected with *P. falciparum* and *P. vivax* erased the malaria symptoms and killed the malaria parasites. Then, on November 8, 1972, Tu also isolated the active ingredient in their extraction. In just over three years, Tu had found and isolated artemisinin, a new compound unlike any known malarial drug, leading to a whole new class of antimalarial drugs. Her work was recognized when she won the 2015 Nobel Prize in Medicine.

To avoid *Plasmodia* surviving artemisinin treatment and becoming resistant to the drug, patients typically take artemisinin with another drug or two that attack the parasite in different ways. Together, these medications are ACTs.

MALARIA IMPACT

Malaria disproportionately affects low-income people, with almost 60 percent of malaria cases occurring among the lowest-income 20 percent of the world's population. In 2022 there were an estimated 249 million malaria cases and 608,000 malaria deaths in eighty-five countries. Ninety-four percent (233 million) of all these malaria cases and 95 percent (580,000) of the malaria deaths were in Africa. Just five central African countries account for 50 percent of all global malarial deaths. The average person is exposed to hundreds of infectious bites yearly in these countries.

In areas where malaria occurs regularly, its fatality rates are the highest for young children who have not yet developed immunity to the disease. For instance, children under five years of age accounted for 80 percent of all malaria deaths in Africa in 2022. In regions where there are sporadic malaria outbreaks, the fatalities due to malaria are spread more evenly across all ages.

As bad as these numbers are, they were worse. The distribution of insecticide-treated nets, safer indoor pesticide sprays, and the adoption of ACTs have accelerated declines in both malaria deaths and infection rates. Thanks to these interventions, global mortality rates declined nearly 40 percent from 2000 to 2015. The pace of improvement has since slowed. In 2020 and 2021, malaria-associated mortality rose due to the disruptions in medical care during the COVID-19 pandemic. Mosquitoes are also adapting to bed nets and indoor spraying. Instead of biting indoors and at night, they are biting outdoors and during the day. But in better news, two new vaccines became available to children living in regions with moderate to high *P. falciparum* transmission in 2023.

MALARIA IN THE FUTURE

As global temperatures rise, malaria's reach will expand, potentially putting over five billion people at risk by 2040. Regions as far north as Alaska and Russia may become hospitable to malaria for part of the year, while areas such as central Australia and southern Africa could see extended transmission seasons. And in high-risk countries such as Uganda and the Democratic Republic of the Congo, malaria cases are projected to increase significantly, with adaptable mosquito species even expanding their transmission to urban areas.

These projections highlight the critical need for proactive measures. Effective combinations of vector control tools—such as insecticidal nets, residual spraying, and genetically modified mosquitoes—could significantly reduce malaria cases. Improved forecasting tools and early-warning systems that monitor climate and socioeconomic trends are also essential, as they empower vulnerable regions to prepare for malaria's shifting threat.

CHAPTER 5

MERS, SARS, COVID-19, AND SPILLOVER

SPILLOVER AND URBANIZATION

Between about 1980 and 2008, thirty new human pathogens emerged. Seventy-five percent of these new diseases were spillover zoonotic diseases.

The rapid and unplanned urban expansion described in chapter 3 often increases contact between humans and the surrounding wildlife, facilitating zoonotic spillover. For instance, the extensive deforestation required to make way for new development narrows the gap between humans and wildlife. Animals living in regions adjacent to towns and cities may be forced to enter built-up areas because their habitats and foraging areas have been reduced. So it is increasingly common to see wild animals—such as bears, baboons, foxes, and birds of prey—scavenging through garbage bins. Such contact raises the risk of disease transmission from these animals to humans and other animals.

SPILLOVER AND WILD ANIMAL TRADE

The encroachment of human civilization into the natural habitats of wild animals also has led to the emergence of a market for cheap meat obtained from hunting animals that live near human settlements. This food source is called bush meat. The hunting, butchering, and sale of the primates, rodents, and reptiles that make up most of the bush meat trade come with a significant risk of exchanging bodily fluids and tissues between the hunter and the hunted. This can facilitate the spillover and spread of new human disease pathogens. Several diseases, including Ebola, avian influenza, HIV, monkeypox virus, anthrax, and COVID-19, have been linked to the sale and consumption of bush meat.

In contrast to local bush meat markets, the long-distance trafficking of wild animals attracts affluent consumers, who pay top dollar for exotic pets, unique luxury foods, and alternative medicines. The international transfer of these exotic, sometimes endangered species is unrelated to urbanization, as the animals are often captured (for the pet trade) and hunted (for the food and medicine trades) far from human settlements.

Most live wildlife illegally transported across borders is destined for the global, multibillion-dollar exotic pet market. The United States is the biggest market for the exotic pet trade—it is worth $15 billion. More than 17.6 million exotic pets are in the United States. Fifty-one percent of these pets are reptiles, birds account for 26 percent, and large mammals including bears, lions, and tigers are imported illegally into the country.

The exotic pet trade has also spread novel diseases from one animal species to another. For instance, one Belgian bird flu outbreak can be traced to mountain eagles smuggled from Thailand to Belgium. The fungal infection chytridiomycosis, which caused the extinction of ninety amphibian species in Australian and Central American rainforests, has been linked to the global trade of African clawed frogs.

While the United States is the largest international market for the exotic pet trade, Asian countries are the most common destination for wildlife sold for fine dining or used for traditional medicine. Pangolins, scaly anteaters from sub-Saharan Africa and Southeast Asia, have become the most trafficked mammals in the world. It is estimated that more than

CONTACT TRACING

Contact tracing is identifying and tracking individuals who might have been exposed to an infectious disease and monitoring them to prevent further infections. It aims to pinpoint and isolate new cases before they transmit the infection, identify and contain outbreaks early, and enhance understanding of how diseases spread. Contact tracing was first used in the 1930s to track syphilis cases. It is fundamental to managing infectious diseases and investigating new or atypical outbreaks. Contact tracing can be instrumental in gathering information when a disease's infectious potential (for example, its reproductive number) is unknown.

After diagnosing a contagious disease, patients collaborate with public health professionals to create a contact list from their infectious period. Health officials then reach out to the listed contacts, alerting them about their potential exposure and advising them on subsequent steps. Identifying and quarantining those who have been in contact with an infected person may help control the spread of the disease. It is also beneficial for those at greater risk of serious illness to get an early warning so they can seek timely medical attention if they develop symptoms.

The complete elimination of smallpox was partly achieved through rigorous contact tracing. Those infected were isolated and at-risk contacts were vaccinated. Contact tracing was also pivotal in the mid-1980s when it provided initial concrete proof that acquired immunodeficiency syndrome (AIDS) could be transmitted sexually.

Contact tracing for SARS was a crucial strategy to end a SARS outbreak in 2003. It was not as effective in limiting the spread of COVID-19 in the 2020s, mainly due to the large number of asymptomatic yet infectious cases that made tracing the path of COVID-19 very difficult.

Scales cover the majority of a pangolin's body. An adult pangolin can have up to one thousand scales.

a million pangolins are caught and killed annually. In Asia, particularly in Vietnam, pangolins are a delicacy in upscale restaurants, selling for up to $150 per 1 pound (0.5 kg). In China, pangolin scales are believed to have medicinal properties. Ground pangolin scales are marketed for a variety of perceived health benefits, such as increasing fertility, promoting lactation, and curing headaches. Although chemically pangolin scales are identical to human fingernails and have no therapeutic properties, they sell for about $6,600 per 1 pound (0.5 kg). Including pangolins and other animals, China's exotic wildlife trade for medical uses and food consumption was worth $73 billion in 2017.

CORONAVIRUSES FROM COLDS TO COVID-19

When observed with an electron microscope, coronaviruses look like the sun's corona (halo), which is how they got their name. Their surfaces are studded with spikes like rays of the sun. These spike projections are the most distinctive feature of coronaviruses. On average, a coronavirus particle has seventy-four surface spikes, which bind to complementary host cell receptors and aid the virus in entering

The coronavirus's spike proteins give it not only its distinct look but also its name.

the host cell. One can think of the spike protein as the key to entering the host cell. They are similar to the hemagglutinins found on the surface of influenza viruses.

Coronaviruses are larger than most viruses found in humans. They also have a much larger genome (they have more genetic information) than most other RNA viruses. The genomes of coronaviruses are three times larger than those of human immunodeficiency virus (HIV) and hepatitis C viruses and twice the size of the influenza virus genome. They can infect both animals and humans.

Coronaviruses are unique among RNA viruses because they possess a genetic proofreading mechanism. This feature ensures that the viral RNA is almost always copied without errors and prevents the accumulation of mutations. This is unusual because mutations are generally beneficial for viral evolution. For instance, influenza viruses mutate three times faster than coronaviruses, allowing them to adapt rapidly and often escape vaccine-induced immunity. But coronaviruses rely on recombination, an exchange of segments of their RNA with other coronaviruses, thereby contributing to their virulence and adaptability. The large viral genome of coronaviruses may be why they need a proofreading system for their genetic material.

SUPER-SPREADERS

Early infectious disease research assumed that all infected individuals had the same likelihood of spreading a contagious disease. That changed between 1900 and 1907 when Mary Mallon infected at least fifty-one individuals with typhoid, three of whom died. She denied being ill because she was asymptomatic. Because her presence was traced back to so many typhoid cases, the New York State Department of Health tested her for *Salmonella typhi*, the bacteria that causes typhoid fever. She tested positive and, in 1907, was forced into quarantine on North Brother Island, between Manhattan and Queens.

Three years later, after many appeals, despite still testing positive, Mallon was released from Brother Island on the condition that she never work as a cook again. But without other job skills, she did not abide by the conditions. She changed her name and worked as a cook. She was still infected and infectious, so she switched jobs whenever typhoid fever struck the family she was working for.

This happened at least seven times before the authorities caught up with her at the Sloane Maternity Hospital in Manhattan, where Mallon was again working as a cook and using the name Mary Brown. During her three months at the maternity ward, she infected twenty-five people, two of whom died. In 1915 she was forced back into quarantine on North Brother Island where she lived until she died of pneumonia on November 11, 1938. Mary Mallon infected at least 122 people, which is significantly higher than expected given that typhoid fever has a reproductive number of three. Mary Mallon is commonly known as Typhoid Mary.

We know that in many infectious diseases, a subset of infected individuals such as Typhoid Mary, termed "super-spreaders," tend to pass on their infections to significantly more people than the average infected person. In most infectious diseases, about 20 percent of those infected account for 80 percent of the disease's spread. This is described as the 80/20 rule, and it has been validated across multiple species and for various pathogens. Simultaneous infection with multiple pathogens, weakened immune systems, asymptomatic infections, air circulation alterations, extensive social and professional networks, and medical care delays can all influence transmission patterns and aid individuals like Typhoid Mary in being or becoming super-spreaders.

Just as specific individuals can lead to significant disease outbreaks, so can certain events. During the COVID-19 pandemic, churches, ski resorts, restaurants, nursing homes, prisons, weddings, funerals, and even Zumba classes acted as super-spreading events.

Contact tracing (see sidebar on page 72) often is used to study super-spreaders and super-spreader events. For example, in 1989 a measles outbreak at a Finnish high school was traced to one individual who transmitted the virus to twenty-two others. Similarly, during an Ebola outbreak in 1995 in Kikwit in the Democratic Republic of the Congo, two individuals showing signs of gastrointestinal bleeding were the probable origin for more than fifty subsequent Ebola infections. And contact tracing of seventy-seven SARS patients during a SARS outbreak in Beijing found that while the majority did not transmit the virus to anyone else, a small number did. Seven patients infected up to three people each, and four were super-spreaders, each passing the virus to at least eight or more people.

Contact tracing and genetic sequencing following the 2020 Biogen conference provide a textbook example of the dangers of a super-spreader event. Biogen is an international biotech company with about 7,500 employees and with headquarters in Cambridge, Massachusetts. In February 2020 the company held a four-day conference at the Marriott Long Wharf hotel in Boston. At the time, COVID-19 was just starting to spread in the United States, with only fifteen confirmed cases nationwide. At the conference, Biogen brought together 175 of its top European and US scientists and administrators. After it ended, reports surfaced that a few people who attended the conference had tested positive for COVID-19 and that seventy of the ninety-two COVID-19 cases diagnosed in Massachusetts were linked to the conference.

Early in the COVID-19 outbreak, researchers analyzed thousands of viral genome sequences from the COVID-19 cases in Massachusetts and across the United States. They identified over eighty distinct SARS-CoV-2 genomes. One of the viral genomes had a unique genetic signature that could be traced to a European attendee at the Biogen conference. The viral sequence was identical to that of the SARS-CoV-2 viruses that were spreading COVID-19 through Europe at the time. But it had an additional single amino acid mutation that must have occurred early in the Biogen conference or on the flight to Boston. This sequence was found only among patients who had direct or indirect contact with attendees of the Biogen conference. By comparing viral sequences

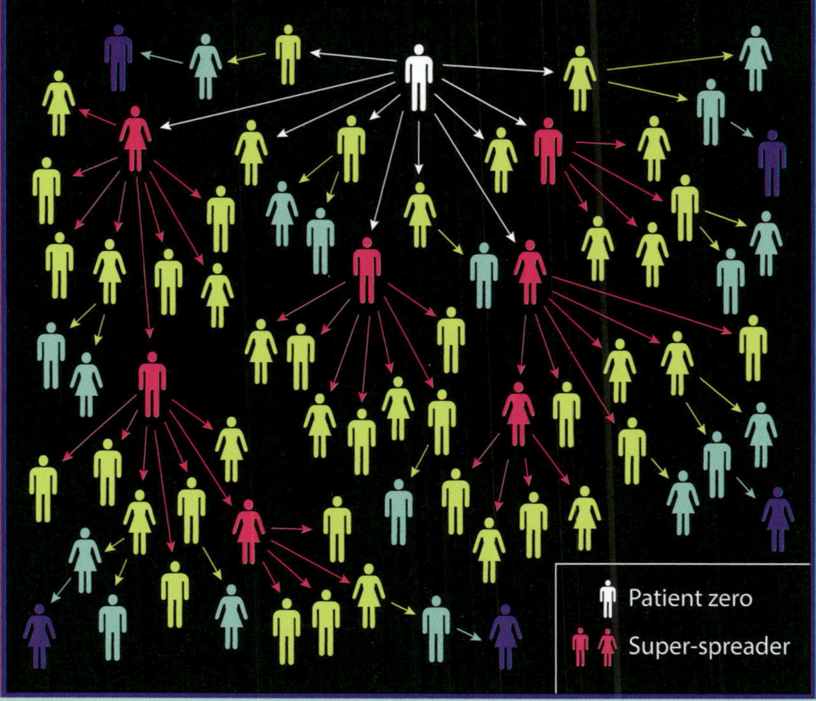

A graphic representing the 2003 Beijing SARS outbreak. This figure demonstrates how just one super-spreading individual can set off a chain reaction that leads to significantly more incidents of the disease.

to a national database, the researchers could track the spread of the Biogen-linked viral strain across the country and internationally. They found this genetic fingerprint in COVID-19 cases in twenty-nine US states and several countries including Australia, Slovakia, and Sweden. This information allowed them to estimate that between 205,000 and 300,000 cases across the United States could be genetically traced to the Biogen conference.

The results of this genetic sequencing and contact tracing illustrate how a mutation acted as a genetic marker, which illuminated the reach and impact of a single super-spreading incident and provided a level of contact tracing not possible through traditional interviews alone. If the mutation had not occurred, no one would have known the extent of the Biogen conference super-spreader event.

CORONAVIRUSES IN ANIMALS AND CORONAVIRUSES CAUSING COLDS IN HUMANS

The first recognized cases of coronavirus infections trace back to the late 1920s when a severe respiratory disease in poultry in North America was recorded. The disease had a mortality rate between 40 percent and 90 percent for newborn chicks. They struggled to breathe and were listless. Scientists Leland David Bushnell and Carl Alfred Brandly isolated the virus responsible for the disease in 1933, and it was named infectious bronchitis virus. Later, in the late 1940s, scientists identified two additional viruses: one causing infection of the brain (murine encephalitis) and the other causing hepatitis in mice. At that time, no one understood the connection between these viruses.

The first human coronavirus was found in the early 1960s. It was isolated in the nasal discharge (mucus) removed from the handkerchiefs of British students suffering from a common cold. Examination under an electron microscope of this virus and a different virus that was also responsible for the common cold in the United States showed that they had a crownlike appearance, with their surfaces covered in spiky protein extensions. These viruses shared the same distinctive appearance as those found in the sick animals in the 1920s. Due to their similarity to the solar corona and one another, in 1968 scientists grouped these viruses together and named them coronaviruses.

There are only four cold coronaviruses (OC43, NL63, 229E, and HKU1), and they are responsible for about 30 percent of all common colds in humans. Before 2003 they were the only human coronaviruses in circulation, and scientists weren't interested in them because the symptoms they produced were so mild. Most coronavirus research focused on animal coronaviruses because they were responsible for severe disease in animals, such as swine (a fatal intestinal illness in young piglets), cattle, horses, camels, cats (high fever and a distended abdomen), dogs, rodents, birds, and bats. Animal coronaviruses often undergo cross-species transmissions. For instance, dog coronaviruses can harm cats, and the cat coronavirus can ravage pig intestines.

Unlike human coronaviruses, they target the gastrointestinal system and spread through fecal-oral routes.

SARS—2003

In the last twenty years, three new coronaviruses have made the leap from animals to humans. Unlike the common cold, which is mild, they have all led to deadly diseases in humans. The first coronavirus to make the transition, SARS-CoV-1, lived in horseshoe bats before passing to Asian palm civets, which are popular in live animal markets, and then to humans. Scientists established this connection in 2003 when they discovered coronaviruses in civets sold in marketplaces in southern China that matched the genetic sequence of the coronaviruses obtained from early human victims of the disease.

The first case of severe acute respiratory syndrome (SARS), the disease caused by the SARS-CoV-1 virus, was recorded in November 2002. A seafood seller with SARS was hospitalized in Guangzhou, China, where he infected numerous doctors and nurses. According to the WHO, a total of 8,098 people in twenty-nine countries became sick with SARS during the 2003 outbreak, and 774 died. The illness was spread through small droplets of saliva. Most patients identified with SARS were previously healthy adults between the ages of twenty-five and seventy years, and the disease killed about one in ten patients.

The virus was aggressive and deadly, with patients typically exhibiting symptoms within two to seven days of exposure. Asymptomatic infections were rare. In response to the SARS outbreak, masks became common, temperature checks were instituted at key public venues throughout China and other Asian regions, and stringent quarantine protocols were enacted. The infection rates reached their peak in late May 2003 before the virus receded. The rigorous enforcement of isolation measures had proved effective, and by July 2003 the WHO announced the end of the crisis. Since 2004 no known cases of SARS have been reported anywhere in the world. After eight months, the pandemic was over. But alarm bells were ringing.

MASKS

Masks play a crucial role in preventing the transmission of respiratory diseases such as the flu, COVID-19, and SARS. They act as a barrier, preventing the spread of respiratory droplets that carry the disease-causing virus. Masks have a dual purpose: They guard the wearer against pathogens that other people emit, and they prevent infected wearers from dispersing respiratory droplets to people nearby.

Cloth masks vary in effectiveness based on the number of layers and fabric type. Proper fit is essential to prevent leakage around the edges of the mask. Cloth masks work through two fundamental principles—they act as a filter, forcing air to weave through fibers where droplets can get trapped, and as a barrier blocking direct transmission of droplets. They typically filter out between 50 and 70 percent of airborne particles.

When it comes to effectiveness, modern masks such as N95 respirators outperform cloth masks. N95 masks filter out at least 95 percent of small airborne particles. They feature a water-repellent (hydrophobic) outer layer to repel respiratory droplets, a middle layer made of tightly woven synthetic fibers with an electrostatic charge that attracts and traps particles more effectively than cloth, and a water-loving (hydrophilic) inner layer that absorbs exhaled respiratory droplets.

Could coronaviruses, which are adept at crossing between animal species and causing severe veterinary disease, spill over into humans and cause more SARS-like diseases?

Researchers collected samples from bats, which harbor many pathogens that frequently result in spillover to humans, and other animals in search of coronaviruses with the potential to infect humans. This extensive effort resulted in the documentation of thousands of viral sequences. There are more than fourteen hundred species of bats, and at least thirty-two hundred coronaviruses affect them. Determining which of these coronaviruses can cross over to humans and then doing something with this information is a challenge, especially since many species, such as the civet, can act as intermediaries between bats and humans.

MERS

On June 13, 2012, a sixty-year-old man was admitted to a hospital in Jeddah, Saudi Arabia. He had acute pneumonia, which progressed to severe respiratory disease, kidney failure, and death. A previously unknown coronavirus that was responsible for his death was isolated from his sputum. Soon, the virus would be found in more patients in the Middle East and in travelers who had been to the region. The virus was named Middle East respiratory syndrome coronavirus (MERS-CoV), and it causes Middle East respiratory syndrome (MERS).

As of August 2023, MERS-CoV has been responsible for 2,605 MERS cases and 937 deaths, with a mortality rate of 37 percent. Genetic sequencing showed that the coronavirus responsible for MERS originated in bats and entered humans from camels. MERS-CoV may have been circulating in camels for two decades before the first recognized case crossed over to humans. The MERS-CoV virus entered the human population multiple times from direct or indirect contact with infected dromedary camels or camel-related products (such as raw camel milk and medicinally used camel urine). Most human infections still come from camels, but some human-to-human transmission has been observed. Since 2020 the number of MERS cases has dropped and has been limited to camel-to-human transmissions in the Arabian Peninsula, with only two new cases reported in 2023 and one in 2024.

COVID-19

In December 2019 a wave of severe and unusual respiratory illnesses hit Wuhan, a city in China with eleven million inhabitants and numerous live animal markets. The disease was soon traced to a new coronavirus, the seventh to cross over from animals to humans. Since it was so closely related to the SARS coronavirus (SARS-CoV) from the 2002–2003 outbreak, the virus was called severe acute respiratory syndrome coronavirus-2 virus, or SARS-CoV-2 for short, and the disease this virus caused would come to be known as COVID-19. Samples taken from raccoon dogs (a type of animal native to eastern Asia), machines that process animals after they have been slaughtered, and cages and drains in the Huanan Seafood Wholesale Market in Wuhan showed that COVID-19 likely arose from a spillover event at this live animal market.

Wuhan is a global travel and commerce hub. Once the spillover event occurred, it didn't take long to crisscross all over China and begin spreading beyond the country's border. The human-to-human transmission of SARS-CoV-2 was efficient. The severity of symptoms ranged from mild to severe. Some individuals, particularly children, were asymptomatic spreaders. Mild symptoms were similar to the flu with an obvious COVID-19 tell, a loss of taste and smell. The severe symptoms included trouble breathing, persistent chest pain, confusion, bluish lips or face, and death.

A few months after declaring a public health emergency on January 30, 2020, the WHO declared COVID-19 a pandemic on March 11, 2020. SARS-CoV-2 had created a global crisis. In the four years after the SARS-CoV-2 virus first turned up in China, more than 770 million individuals worldwide were infected by the virus, causing more than seven million deaths.

SARS-COV-2

All seven coronaviruses that infect humans lead to respiratory disease. Three of them, SARS-CoV, SAR-CoV-2, and MERS-CoV, lead to severe and often fatal diseases with fatality rates of 10 percent, 5 percent, and 36 percent, respectively. The other four lead to mild symptoms associated with the common cold. Those four typically lead to upper respiratory tract infections (nose and throat). SARS-CoV and MERS-CoV rarely cause such infections. Instead, they tend to infect the lungs. This is why SARS and MERS are more deadly than the common cold but are not very infectious and can be controlled by isolation, masking, and quarantine. SARS-CoV-2 is a fatal mix of both groups, and it efficiently infects both the upper respiratory tract and the lungs. This dual ability allows SARS-CoV-2 to combine the widespread infectiousness of coughing and sneezing typical of common cold coronaviruses with the deadly nature of MERS-CoV and SARS-CoV.

SARS-CoV-2 enters the body through droplets from an infected person's nose and mouth. It uses its spike proteins to recognize and bind to receptors on its victims' cells. This helps the virus fuse to the host cell membrane and enter the cell. Although the spike proteins are similar across all human coronaviruses, the spike proteins of the cold virus bind to cells in the throat and nose, while those of the SARS and MERS viruses only bind to receptors on cells in the lower respiratory tract. Meanwhile, the spike protein of SARS-CoV-2 differs from those found on the coronaviruses that cause the common cold. As a result, the antibodies developed against common cold coronaviruses are ineffective in preventing or mitigating the symptoms of COVID-19.

The cells infected in the respiratory tract die once the initial SARS-CoV-2 virus has produced hundreds of new viral offspring, which break out of the infected cells and go on to invade new neighboring cells and move farther into the lungs. In a few days, there are millions of SARS-CoV-2 viruses. Symptoms of the disease are mild until the immune system is activated. Once the immune system kicks in, the virus becomes a smaller part of the disease. At this stage, the symptoms are caused by the immune system's response rather than the virus itself. They are much more severe than those that the virus causes and result in significant host-tissue damage.

Modern research shows that one of the cold viruses, OC43, may once have been more deadly than it is now. Genetic sequencing suggests that OC43, not an influenza virus, was responsible for the 1889–1890 Russian flu pandemic. In 1889, shortly after it transferred from mice to cows and then to humans, coronavirus OC43 killed over one million people. Antibodies against the virus were found in the dental pulp of World War I soldiers who had been alive during the Russian flu and fell in battle in 1914.

Many researchers believe that all four cold-causing coronaviruses started as lethal human pathogens. They were novel viruses like SARS-CoV and SARS-CoV-2 and caused severe infections because they were unknown to the human immune system. Then they evolved into infectious but less severe common cold coronaviruses. If that theory is correct, then COVID-19 is here to stay, and it will slowly mutate into another one of the cold viruses.

VARIANTS

Viruses are nothing more than molecular machines designed to get a host cell to make new viruses using the instructions encoded in the virus's RNA or DNA. To keep track of the spread and changing features of COVID-19, facilities all over the world sequence the coronavirus RNA obtained from nasal swabs of COVID-19 patients. This genomic surveillance has led to the collection of an unprecedented volume of genomic data for a single pathogen. It has allowed researchers to observe evolutionary developments such as the rise of virus variants that exhibit specific traits including increased transmissibility, greater severity of disease, and the ability to evade immune responses in real time.

Most SARS-CoV-2 sequences are uploaded into international databases. The Global Initiative on Sharing All Influenza Data

(GISAID) platform is one of these. It has over 16.5 million SARS-CoV-2 genetic sequences submitted from 241 countries and territories. Visualization tools, such as the open-source platform Nextstrain, allow people to view the sequences, maps of disease spread, and more.

After eight months of the pandemic, SARS-CoV-2 underwent evolutionary shifts, leading to the emergence of mutated forms with increased transmissibility. Because of the spike proteins' importance in binding to the correct host cells in the nose, bronchi, and lungs and in entering these cells, mutations in the sequence of the nucleotides that encode for these proteins were among the most significant mutations found in the new variants. The mutations contributed to the variants' ability to evade immunity and sustain high transmission rates among populations that were previously immune to the old forms of COVID-19. The variants arose independently in different global locations, and each outperformed their predecessors to become the dominant strains in various regions worldwide.

To simplify the discussion and make public communication about variants easier and less confusing, the WHO gives new variants Greek letter names when they are substantially different from existing variants in severity, immune evasion, or transmission. As of late 2024, the alpha, beta, delta, and omicron variants have been the most significant.

Early in the COVID pandemic, mutations occurred at about two mutations per month, a slow evolution like that of the other six coronaviruses. But since then, the evolutionary pace of SARS-CoV-2 has accelerated to the rates observed in the influenza A virus. The variants most likely develop in immunocompromised patients with repeated and persistent COVID-19 infections, as this is the perfect environment for selecting SARS-CoV-2 variants that can rapidly replicate and evade the weakened immune system.

No evidence suggests that recombination was involved in the origin of any of the variants, including omicron. But recombination remains a continuing source of concern, mainly as human-to-animal spillover

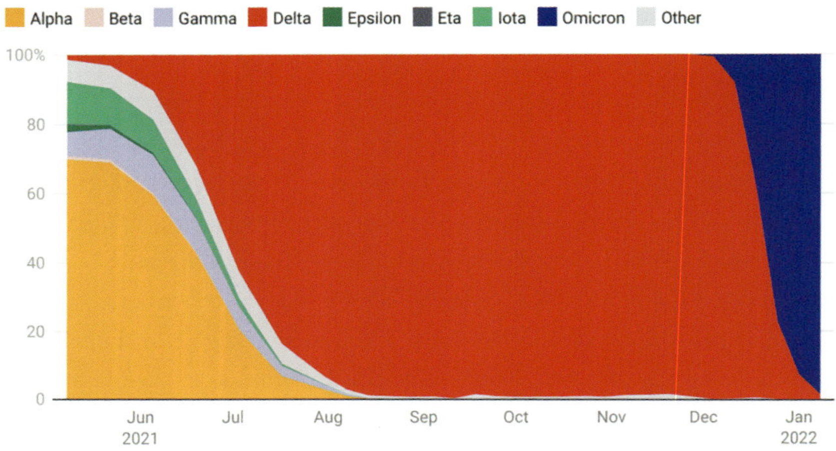

COVID-19 variant prevalence in the United States. If this graph was continued to the end of 2024, it would show much more blue, as omicron has been the sole variant present since January 2022.

has been observed in cats, dogs, farmed minks, and lions and tigers in zoos. Scientists worry the human SARS-CoV-2 may evolve, perhaps by recombination with animal coronaviruses, in an animal host before transmission back to a human host.

WHERE IS COVID-19 NOW?

The emergence of the omicron variant in autumn 2021 marked the beginning of a new phase of the COVID-19 pandemic. Omicron had many new mutations, including thirty-seven changes on its spike protein. It is more infectious, with a shorter doubling time than previous variants, and it has a greater ability to infect patients who have had COVID-19 before. It replaced the previously dominant delta variant in just a few weeks and has remained the only variant found in patients since, although new versions (called lineages) of omicron constantly pop up. Fortunately, the symptoms of omicron are less severe than those of all the other variants of SARS-CoV-2. This is because some of the spike mutations reduce omicron's capacity to spread into the lower respiratory tract.

COVID-19 VACCINES—WHERE ARE WE NOW?

In 2020 strict measures such as social distancing, travel restrictions, quarantining, and masking were enforced worldwide to tackle the pandemic. These measures were designed to slow the spread of the virus. Scientists understood that to control the pandemic, they needed an effective vaccine and some luck (such as a variant that had a diminished capacity to spread to the lower respiratory tract of its human host).

As we've discussed, vaccines work by stimulating the immune system to produce an immune response against a disease without causing the disease. They contain weakened or inactive parts of a specific pathogen that trigger an immune response to the disease of interest. This response leads to the production of antibodies and the development of memory cells, which provide immunity against the disease. When a vaccinated person is later exposed to the pathogen, their immune system can recognize and destroy it, preventing or mitigating the disease. Vaccines help the body learn how to defend itself against a disease without the dangers of a full-blown infection.

COVID-19 vaccines train the immune system to recognize and fight the SARS-CoV-2 virus. They use the spike protein of SARS-CoV-2 to stimulate vaccinated patients' immune systems, which create antibodies and defensive white blood cells to fight any pathogen with similar spike proteins. Some vaccines use a weakened version of the disease-causing pathogen to prime the host immune system. But the most common COVID-19 vaccines use just the spike protein or pieces of the spike protein to trick the immune system into thinking that a coronavirus is threatening it.

The two main types of COVID-19 vaccines are messenger RNA (mRNA) and viral vector vaccines.

In mRNA vaccines, mRNA segments that encode for the SARS-CoV-2 virus's spike protein are enclosed in lipid nanoparticles and injected into muscles. The muscle cells use the instructions encoded in the mRNA to synthesize the spike protein, prompting the body to develop antibodies against it. After the cells have produced the spike protein segments, they break down the mRNA as cells do after making proteins. The mRNA does not cause a COVID-19 infection. The mRNA COVID-19 vaccine was the first mRNA vaccine ever approved and used by health authorities all over the world.

In vector vaccines, a different, harmless virus is used as a vector to carry the genetic blueprint for creating the SARS-CoV-2 spike protein to your cells. Upon expression of the spike protein on the vector's exterior, the immune system is triggered to produce antibodies and white blood cells as a defense mechanism against any viruses with a similar spike protein. Should you later encounter the COVID-19 virus, these antibodies are prepared to engage it. These vaccines also do not cause COVID-19.

Scientists developed the COVID-19 vaccines in record time. It took less than twelve months from the moment SARS-CoV-2 was isolated before scientists began testing the safety and effectiveness of the COVID-19 vaccines so they could be provided to the public. The previous record for developing a vaccine for a new disease was four years, and the average time to make a vaccine is twelve years. One must admire both the speed of the vaccine development and its subsequent manufacture and distribution. In just three years, 13.6 billion COVID-19 vaccine doses were administered, and 67 percent of the world's population had at least one shot.

Both the United States and the WHO ended their states of emergency in May 2023. They did so in part because the omicron variant, the only variant presently detected in humans, is less likely to cause the more harmful infections of the lower respiratory tract.

And most people on Earth have partial immunity to the SARS-CoV-2 virus because they have had at least one bout of COVID-19 or have had one or more COVID-19 vaccinations. This partial immunity is not perfect, and many people still get COVID-19. But they tend to get the initial COVID-19 symptoms associated with the viral damage of the SARS-CoV-2 and not the harmful host tissue damage caused by the activated immune system in the secondary stage of COVID-19. In 2025 COVID-19 is no longer a public health emergency and is considered endemic by most experts.

CHAPTER 6

THE INFODEMIC AND MISINFORMATION

In 2003, long before the COVID pandemic, the WHO coined the term *infodemic*. An infodemic is an overabundance of information, including false and misleading information, during an epidemic. It causes confusion that can harm public health and lead to mistrust of health authorities.

The scale of the infodemic associated with the COVID-19 pandemic was unprecedented. Traditional media (newspapers and television) and social media including Facebook, X (formerly Twitter), and WhatsApp produced so much COVID-related information that it was impossible to parse and fact-check even a fraction of it. In February 2020 Tedros Adhanom Ghebreyesus, director-general of the WHO, was forced to warn the world, "We're not just fighting an epidemic; we're fighting an infodemic. Fake news spreads faster and more easily than the virus, and it is just as dangerous. . . . This is a time for facts, not fear. This is a time for rationality, not rumors. This is a time for solidarity, not stigma."

Infodemics behave similar to infectious diseases. They start locally and then spread globally (go viral). Super-spreaders (celebrities, influencers, and high-level politicians) only produce 20 percent of all misinformation, but it spreads and accounts for about 70 percent of all misinformation. Contact tracing is used to find the source of misinformation (see vaccines in the Misinformation to Sow Discord section on page 93). People have different susceptibilities to misinformation (older adults, those with fewer years of formal education, and those on the political extremes are the most susceptible). Spillover occurs (misinformation can start on Facebook and end up on TV, X, or other sites). And the consequences can be severe (about 319,000 deaths between January 2021 and April 2022 could have been prevented if the individuals had been vaccinated).

A global risks perception survey of 1,490 world leaders from civil society, business, academia, and government ranked misinformation (wrong information accidentally created) and disinformation (incorrect information purposely created and spread) together as the most significant short-term risk for 2024 to 2026, with extreme weather events coming in second.

Disease-related misinformation is not new. It has been around as long as people have spread news. During the Black Death, no one knew what caused the plague and how it spread. The event was a breeding ground for rumors (misinformation) and lies (disinformation). In the spring of 1348, in southern France and northern Spain, rumors started appearing that Jewish communities were poisoning water wells and that they were the source of the plague. These lies were accompanied by violence against Jews and spread across the German-speaking world as fast as the plague itself. More than two hundred Jewish communities were destroyed not by the Black Death but because of anti-Semitic lies associated with the pandemic.

The internet, artificial intelligence (AI), and social media have changed how misinformation and disinformation are created and spread. The internet, and social media in particular, have become the go-to medical information sources, especially among teenagers and young adults. The line between health news, knowledge, and entertainment has disappeared, which has devalued the importance of facts and given us the illusion of being informed. Health information is often shared through entertaining formats such as videos and memes. This can make the information easier to understand but may leave out important details. Then it is harder to tell the difference between reliable information and opinions or unproven claims.

Oversimplified content can make some people think they understand complex topics better than they do. They may also feel more knowledgeable than they are because there's so much health information online. The internet has increased the volume of information across decades. In 1994 there were fewer than three thousand websites. Now, there are over 1.5 billion, although fewer than 200 million are active. Thanks to the internet, we have instant access to more medical news and information than ever before. But the accuracy of medical information online is inconsistent, and it is difficult to recognize misinformation and disinformation.

Meanwhile, people use large AI language models such as ChatGPT to create new websites, magazine articles, and even books. These tools are far from perfect and can introduce misinformation if not carefully curated. Artificial intelligence can also be used to introduce disinformation and false photos purposely.

You probably want to know why someone would deliberately spread false medical information. There are many reasons, the most common of which are to sell unproven medical products, sow discord, create political advantage, and get new followers.

SOCIAL MEDIA—SUPER-SPREADER

The internet and especially social media websites have magnified neighborhood gossip. During the Black Death, person-to-person contact propagated rumors, which limited both the speed and area of the spread of the rumors. But as of February 2025, 68 percent of the global population (more than 5 billion people) use social media. The largest social media platform is Facebook with over 3 billion monthly users. YouTube comes in second with 2.5 billion active users, followed by WhatsApp (about 3 billion), Instagram (2 billion), and TikTok (1.6 billion). This unprecedented connectivity has the potential to spread health and medical misinformation further than ever.

Research has shown that fake news spreads faster and further than the truth. We have often seen and heard the truth before, but misinformation and disinformation are new to us. They pique our interest, and we are more likely to like or repost the false information.

Social media networks, especially platforms with vast user bases such as Facebook, are increasingly plagued by fake accounts, which undermine authentic interactions and pose significant challenges to digital spaces. An estimated 270 million Facebook accounts are either bots or fake profiles. Bots are automated computer programs designed to spread disinformation, influence political conversations, manipulate public opinion, and spread discord through social media networks. Bots are also common on all the other social media platforms.

MISINFORMATION TO SOW DISCORD

Scientific consensus says that smoking causes lung cancer, that genetically modified foods are healthy, that global warming and climate change are real, and that vaccines protect us from infectious diseases without causing autism, attention deficit hyperactivity disorder, epilepsy, diabetes, or any other conditions. This has not stopped anti-vaccine activists, often called anti-vaxxers.

Like an epidemiologist tracking the transmission of a new virus, researchers have dug deep to establish the origin of extreme pro- and anti-vaccine tweets posted before the COVID-19 pandemic started. They discovered that the vast majority of the extreme vaccine tweets, pro and con, came from the same set of Russian bot accounts. The tweets were written to increase the polarization of American society by using divisive language linking vaccination to social and racial disparities. They were successful in part because anti-vaxxers changed their focus from "vaccines don't work and are bad for you" to a more politically orientated platform that argued that vaccines infringe on our medical freedoms, that the decision to receive vaccines is a personal choice and should not be influenced by external forces, that the government should not have the authority to dictate what we can or cannot inject into our own bodies or the bodies of our kids, and that we as individuals have the right to make these decisions for ourselves. These ideas appealed to the political right as well as some wellness and health supplement companies.

During the COVID pandemic, vaccination became a bigger issue, and many people did not get vaccinated against the disease despite all the medical evidence in favor of getting COVID-19 vaccinations. Medical freedom became an even stronger part of the Republican identity. In July 2021, Democrats were 20 percent more likely to be vaccinated than Republicans.

Researchers at the University of California, Davis, have shown that individuals who consume large amounts of news on social media and less mainstream media are more likely to be skeptical of COVID-19 vaccines and exhibit greater hesitation about vaccination. This shows how social media can make a sensitive topic worse by reinforcing extreme points of view, and it is an example of social media being used as a geopolitical weapon to sow discord and disrupt public health efforts.

MISINFORMATION FOR FINANCIAL GAIN

Anti-vaccine misinformation is not only distributed to sow discord but also for profit. Despite some flagging it as misinformation, large social media companies do not remove anti-vaccine content because it is good for business. Anti-vaxxers have a devoted following and reach up to fifty-eight million online supporters. Researchers traced the source of anti-vaccination misinformation and found that since the start of the COVID-19 pandemic, most posts originate from and are funded by wellness and supplement companies, who directly profit from anti-vaccination campaigns by offering "healthy" alternatives to vaccines.

Using health misinformation to make money is nothing new. In 1672 Robert Talbor, a self-educated doctor, was appointed royal physician by King Charles II because he was able to manipulate prejudice to his advantage. As we have seen earlier in this book, during Talbor's lifetime, a drink made from the bark of the cinchona tree was the best defense against malaria. But Protestant countries (England, the Netherlands, and Germany) were reluctant to use the anti-malaria tincture due to its association with Catholicism. Talbor devised an alternative. He sold a cinchona, wine, and opium mixture that disguised the bitter taste of the bark, was a little addictive, and still effectively treated malaria. Although it was from the same substance, he sold the treatment as a safe substitute for the Jesuits' bark with no Catholic association.

Talbor's secret anti-malaria remedy was a great success. In 1678 he was knighted. King Louis XIV of France paid Talbor three thousand gold crowns and gave him a title. In return, Talbor promised to reveal the secret formula of his anti-malaria medicine upon his death. In 1681 Talbor died at the age of thirty-nine, and in the next year, Talbor's secret treatment was revealed. The English translation of the remedy was titled "The English Remedy: Or Talbor's Wonderful Secret for the Curing of Agues and Fevers—Sold by the Author, Sir Robert Talbor, to the Most Christian King and Since His Death Ordered by His Majesty to Be Published in French, for the Benefit of His Subjects."

MISINFORMATION TO GET MORE FOLLOWERS, AS ENTERTAINMENT, OR FOR POLITICAL GAIN

Quinine is the active ingredient in the cinchona bark concoction that Talbor sold. Hydroxychloroquine is a drug that was first synthesized in 1946. It is structurally like quinine, and like quinine, it is used as an antimalarial agent and has been at the center of a medical misinformation scandal.

Early in the COVID-19 pandemic, researchers were looking for treatments that could be effectively used against the SARS-CoV-2 virus. No one knew much about COVID-19, other than that it was a new disease caused by a coronavirus, so no specific treatment was available. Initial in vitro tests (tests conducted in a petri dish, not in a model organism) with hydroxychloroquine showed that the drug inhibited SARS-CoV-2 replication in some cells. Normally, drugs that have shown positive in vitro results progress to testing in animal models before advancing to larger clinical trials with humans. Novel disease pandemics such as COVID-19 aren't normal, and many shortcuts are taken in such desperate times.

On March 16, 2020, the results of a study on the use of hydroxychloroquine in patients with SARS-CoV-2 were released via YouTube, a highly unusual way of "publishing" scientific and medical results. It was a very small study, with just twenty-six COVID-19 patients receiving hydroxychloroquine. The authors reported that the treatment resulted in the patients getting better faster and being contagious for a shorter time than the patients not receiving hydroxychloroquine.

Medicinal chemists and medical doctors were suspicious of the results because they were not obtained through randomized, controlled clinical trials. They advocated for rapid, large-scale, placebo-controlled clinical studies to confirm the results. In a placebo-controlled trial, some participants would receive the hydroxychloroquine treatment while others receive a treatment lacking the hydroxychloroquine, the placebo. The most reliable trials are also double-blind (neither the researchers nor the volunteers know who receives the active medication or the placebo).

But celebrities and politicians were not concerned by the lack of standard clinical studies and supported the studies online and on television. Dr. Oz of *The Dr. Oz Show* endorsed the unproven findings. On April 4, 2020, then-US President Donald Trump, "speaking on gut instinct," authorized an emergency override of standard Food and Drug Administration (FDA) regulations for the treatment of COVID-19 with hydroxychloroquine and chloroquine. This allowed

The Dr. Oz Show, which often featured health products or tips that had little to no scientific evidence proving they were useful or prevented disease, ended in 2022. Mehmet Oz (*right*), popularly known as Dr. Oz, was then sworn in as the administrator for the Centers for Medicare and Medicaid Services in 2025, under the second Trump administration.

the US government to purchase and stockpile twenty-nine million hydroxychloroquine tablets for COVID-19 patients even though the drug's efficacy had not been fully tested.

The consequence of the publicity and the FDA emergency override was that many patients pressured their doctors to prescribe hydroxychloroquine pills for COVID-19 treatment, even though there was little evidence to support their use. And many productive studies on other potential COVID-19 treatments had to be stopped and repurposed to study hydroxychloroquine since research resources were limited. In addition to the suspension of some promising avenues of COVID-19 research, some malaria patients were denied proper treatment as hydroxychloroquine, commonly used to treat certain forms of malaria, became scarce due to its widespread use in treating COVID-19.

Over three months, researchers completed dozens of randomized, controlled trials of hydroxychloroquine with tens of thousands of patients. The trials all showed that hydroxychloroquine did not effectively treat COVID-19, did not decrease the infection rate of people with COVID-19, and led to serious heart problems in some people. The FDA had collected enough information and ended the emergency regulations that allowed for hydroxychloroquine and chloroquine to be used in the treatment of COVID-19. But by that time, more than one million Americans had taken hydroxychloroquine pills.

MISINFORMATION AND COVID-19

The hydroxychloroquine story is just one example of many that highlight the distribution of misinformation and its consequences during the COVID-19 pandemic. The danger of vaccines, the use of ivermectin as a COVID-19 treatment, 5G networks causing COVID-19, the use of masks, and the numerous origin stories of COVID-19 are a few other examples of "fake news" that made global headlines. They confused all of us and caused many of us to lose faith in science, the CDC, and the FDA.

COVID-19 has taught us a lot about infodemics. During the COVID-19 pandemic, people were spending more time at home and searching online for answers to an uncertain and rapidly changing situation. The problem was the answers they were getting were incorrect. For instance, on Twitter, almost 42 percent of over 178 million COVID-19-related tweets were produced by bots, and 40 percent were "unreliable." But over 54 percent of American adults still get their news from social media.

Some of the misinformation is ridiculous, and some is dangerous. It is spread to gain political advantage, out of xenophobic (fear of foreigners) spite or to cause other harm, or it can be well intentioned but misguided health advice. In 2020 hundreds of Iranians died after drinking methanol because they believed it would protect them from the virus. In a small Ukrainian town, violence erupted after it was rumored that a plane carrying COVID-19 patients had arrived from Wuhan. Meanwhile, in the United Kingdom, 5G telephone masts were burned after Facebook and Twitter were abuzz with claims that 5G Wi-Fi networks were responsible for COVID-19. Influencers and celebrities such as actor Woody Harrelson and singer M.I.A. promoted the 5G theory.

The arrival of a new life-threatening disease made us desperate for information. But, by its nature, science rarely offers a quick fix. New technologies and medicines often take years to prove they are safe and effective. The SARS-CoV-2 virus was new to science. This means we didn't understand many aspects of its spread, and scientists proposed many conflicting theories and models that had to be proved or disproved. This is how science works.

This seeming lack of scientific consensus fertilized the growth of many conspiracy theories and false health advice. In the information vacuum, other less reliable sources, such as celebrities and politicians, spread unsubstantiated rumors. At the start of the COVID pandemic, virologists, epidemiologists, and emergency room physicians were too busy to give interviews, and most of our information came from self-proclaimed experts—business school professors, economists, and celebrities selling wellness products. Misinformation was everywhere. The source of medical information should have been trusted medical and scientific journals (the so-called peer-reviewed journals), not YouTube videos, wellness companies, or TV morning shows.

THE FUTURE OF MEDICAL MISINFORMATION

Medical misinformation is likely to remain a significant challenge in the near future, especially as social media continues to be a primary channel for spreading false health information. With the ease of sharing content and algorithms favoring engaging (but often misleading) posts, we can expect to see an increase in AI-generated content, sophisticated "deepfake" videos, and images that appear to support unverified medical claims. This will complicate efforts to control misinformation while respecting free speech.

And misinformation will likely spread beyond vaccines to new health topics, including emerging diseases, climate impacts on health, and advancements in medical technology such as gene editing and AI. In response, health organizations, tech companies, and governments will likely invest more in digital literacy programs, develop AI tools to detect misinformation, and possibly introduce new regulations aimed at reducing health misinformation online. But the impact on public health could be significant, from continued vaccine hesitancy to delays in proper medical care and growing distrust in health institutions. Combating misinformation will require ongoing collaboration, vigilance, and education to mitigate its harmful effects and ensure the public has access to reliable, evidence-based information.

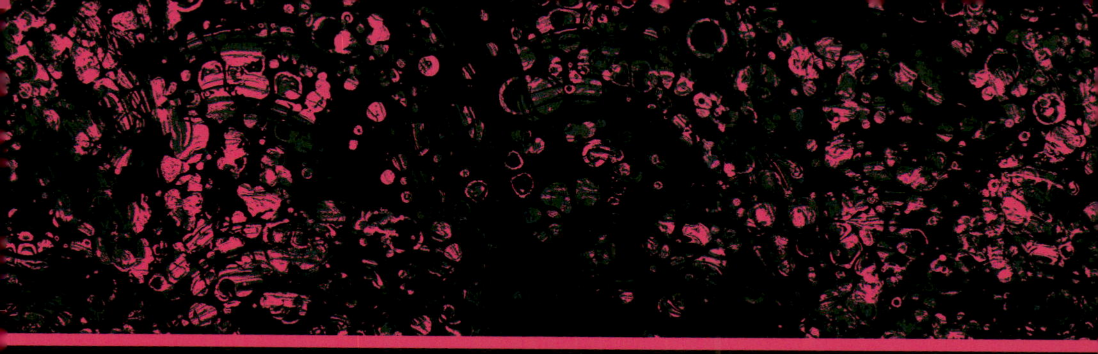

CONCLUSION

HOW PREPARED WILL WE BE FOR THE NEXT PANDEMIC?

Viruses and bacteria were well established on Earth billions of years before mammals appeared. Our survival and progress as a species have been contingent on our ability to live in harmony with these microorganisms and to fend off those that are detrimental to our well-being. These are the pathogens that cause infectious diseases.

Throughout human history, pathogens and the diseases they cause have posed a constant threat to our species. During the era of hunter-gatherers, which lasted from around 2.6 million years ago until about 10,000 years ago, disease outbreaks were typically confined to a single area. And if they did happen to spread, it was usually at a slow pace. But, with the advent of agriculture around 12,000 years ago, humans and animals began to interact more closely. This led to the transmission of animal diseases to humans and the emergence of new diseases. Meanwhile, the widespread trade associated with increased agriculture drove people to expand their horizons—and infectious diseases traveled with them.

Some of the proof that the conversion from a hunting and gathering society to an agrarian one led to an increase in infectious diseases has come from archaeologists. They discovered evidence showing that after the switch to agriculture, the percentage of child and adolescent skeletons they found was much higher than during hunting and gathering times. Adults would have developed some immunity to these new diseases, while children and adolescents were more susceptible to them. Research also showed that most of the changes in the fifteen hundred genes responsible for protecting us from diseases occurred in the last six thousand to thirteen thousand years, which was when our ancestors switched to agriculture.

In the last century, the same driving forces that led to an increase in disease outbreaks twelve thousand years ago were supercharged by technological advances that changed the way new infectious diseases appear and spread across the world.

For many years, experts in virology and epidemiology have warned us about the possibility of a viral outbreak like the COVID-19 pandemic. Despite these warnings, we were not adequately prepared for COVID-19, and public officials could not agree on the best course of action. We faced shortages of critical medical equipment, such as ventilators and surgical masks, and experienced other problems that were not directly related to public health, including increased political divisions, supply chain issues, and disruptions to education.

SCIENCE AND TECHNOLOGY

Science and technology have changed how we approach and experience diseases, transforming everything from diagnosis and treatment to prevention and patient care. Advances in medical research allow scientists to understand the genetic and molecular bases of diseases, leading to targeted therapies that were unimaginable a few decades ago.

Smallpox caused widespread death and suffering for tens of thousands of years and claimed the lives of billions of people. In just the last century of its existence, up to three hundred million people died from smallpox. Fortunately, vaccines proved to be effective in defeating the disease, and as a result, the WHO declared smallpox eradicated in 1980.

During the eighteenth and nineteenth centuries, people commonly experienced outbreaks of diseases including cholera, measles, smallpox, typhoid, and yellow fever. Such outbreaks were considered a normal part of life. Our ancestors relied on their immune systems to combat pathogens. Today, we enlist science and medicine to support our body's defense systems.

Advances in science and medicine vanquished smallpox and helped diminish the fatalities associated with other common epidemics and pandemics. For instance, the increase in the average mortality rate due to the 1849 cholera epidemic was 69 percent, and the 1918 flu caused a 38 percent increase in the rate of mortality, but COVID-19 was responsible for a mortality that was "only" 15 percent above normal. Early detection of disease outbreaks, vaccines, medicines, rapid vaccine development, and improved diagnosis help protect us from the effects of diseases, especially novel ones.

While advances in science and technology protect us from the ravages of pandemics, they also increase the likelihood of new pandemics. An investigation of disease outbreaks in the last four centuries revealed that the probability of new pandemics has increased by several times due to human advancements. The growth of live animal markets that can act as viral mixing bowls (spillover—chapter 4), increased world travel (human mobilization—chapter 2), increasing population density (global urbanization—chapter 3), climate change (climate change—chapter 5), and infodemics (misinformation—chapter 6) have made new pandemics pretty much inevitable.

These forces are resulting in new infectious diseases popping up at an unprecedented rate all over the world. In 1976 in a small village on the Ebola River in Zaire (now the Democratic Republic of the Congo), one of the deadliest viral diseases, Ebola fever, was discovered. In the mid-1970s, Zaire also was dealing with a new disease that caused its victims to waste away. They called it slim disease, and it was the forerunner of HIV-AIDS. SARS and COVID-19 appeared in China (2003 and 2019, respectively), Zika in Uganda (1947), and MERS in Saudi Arabia (2012).

So, unfortunately, there will be other pandemics. To mitigate them, we must empower science and medicine to treat new diseases and limit their spread.

MISINFORMATION

Despite all the advances in science, when a new disease infects people for the first time, scientists and medical doctors don't know how to treat it or prevent its spread. They have to use best practices based on similar previously observed diseases. Experts often have different opinions because all the facts aren't known at the time. It takes hard work and many scientific experiments to discover the life cycle, weaknesses, and ins and outs of the infective behavior of a new pathogen.

The public and the press must realize it is OK for science and medicine to be wrong during the start of novel disease outbreaks. They should expect the scientific and medical community to change recommendations when new data is available. And they should try not to lose trust or confidence in science and medicine, which is difficult because the beginning of new, unknown disease outbreaks can be volatile and stressful. But we can expect a scientific consensus only once all the experiments have been done and all the data has been evaluated.

Conspiracy theories are made up and much easier to create, spread, and understand than new scientific theories. This is why disease outbreaks are often associated with waves of rumors and misinformation that result in distrust and antagonism of public health authorities such as the CDC and the WHO. We will have to distinguish between the uncertainty and change associated with early research of new diseases and the medical misinformation and conspiracy theories.

VACCINATIONS

The larger the reproductive number of a disease is, the greater the fraction of the population that has to be vaccinated, masked, isolated, or a combination of these to stop the spread of the disease. So a sizable portion of the public must be willing, or be mandated, to adopt preventive measures, resulting in friction between legislating adherence to the measures or allowing the public the medical freedom to choose their treatment or lack thereof, even if they are responding to misinformation.

In 1777, during the Revolutionary War (1775–1783), George Washington, then commander in chief of the Continental Army, ordered the inoculation (an early form of vaccination) of the army against smallpox after recognizing its importance in keeping his forces healthy and ready for battle. It was remarkably effective and is often presented as one of the first US vaccine mandates.

CHILD MORTALITY RATE, INCLUDING UNITED NATIONS PROJECTIONS

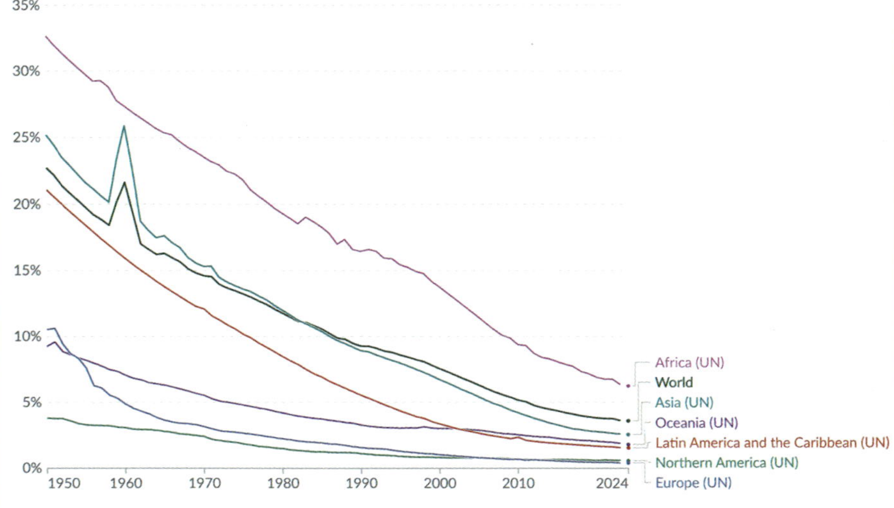

The child mortality rate has steadily decreased with time. This is in part because, in the last fifty years, immunization has reduced infant mortality by 40 percent.

In 1809 Massachusetts became the first state in the United States to pass a law requiring smallpox vaccination, setting a precedent that several other states soon followed. This early effort to mandate vaccination faced strong opposition, leading many states to repeal their laws. The objections to vaccination were rooted in religious beliefs, sanitary concerns, and political views—arguments that still resonate two centuries later.

Although COVID-19 vaccines provide substantial protection against severe illness, hospitalization, and death, 81 percent of the US population has received at least one COVID-19 vaccine, but only 70 percent are considered fully vaccinated. During the COVID-19 pandemic, anti-vaccination fears came from a mistrust of science, the government, and the pharmaceutical industry, in addition to baseless concerns that vaccines cause autism or infertility. These fears have been mainly spread by social media accounts in an attempt to sell alternative unproven COVID-19 wellness products (such as probiotics and elderberry), supplements (such as zinc and vitamins C and D), and homeopathic products (such as *Gelsemium sempervirens* and *Bryonia alba*). As we continue to combat misinformation, it is essential for individuals to rely on credible, science-based sources and to make informed decisions that protect their health and the health of their communities.

MASKING

Plague doctors believed that miasma was responsible for the plague. To protect themselves, they wore masks stuffed with fragrant herbs. The masks worked because they prevented the airborne *Y. pestis* from passing through, protecting the doctors from the pneumatic form of the plague.

By the time the 1918 influenza made its appearance, germ theory was well established, and doctors knew that they could protect themselves from the flu viruses by wearing masks. But their cloth masks weren't remarkably effective and required multiple cloth layers to work.

On October 22, 1918, San Francisco was the first US city to mandate that residents wear four-layer masks in public spaces. Jail sentences of up to ten days were imposed on San Franciscans who did not comply with the masking rules. After a month, the masking regulations in San Francisco were relaxed because the number of new flu cases had dropped to six per day. With no masking mandates in place, it took less than three weeks for the infection rates to rise to over three hundred per day. The health department advocated for a reimposition of mask mandates, but business groups and citizens who believed that the masking rules infringed on their civil liberties blocked them.

During the COVID-19 pandemic, we saw similar arguments between those advocating for mandated vaccinations, masking, and isolation and those who believed such mandates would infringe on their individual freedoms. Due to these arguments, around thirty states passed legislation that prevents public health authorities from enacting protective measures without approval from the state legislature. These laws will put those states at a severe disadvantage when the next major disease outbreak comes, as mandates can be essential tools to protect public health by ensuring swift, coordinated action to prevent widespread illness and save lives.

We must be ready to negotiate the inevitable tension between public health and individual civil rights when another pandemic arrives.

INEQUITIES

There is still a significant disease burden gap between wealthier, industrialized countries and lower-income, less industrialized countries. This is why child mortality in sub-Saharan Africa is more than fourteen times higher than in Europe and North America.

COVID-19 vaccine distribution is another example of international health inequities. By the end of 2021, most people in Europe and North America had received their first COVID-19 shots, while less than 5 percent of the population in sub-Saharan Africa had been vaccinated. This was not due to a global lack of vaccines but rather the result of wealthier nations hoarding vaccine quantities far beyond their needs, leaving a surplus of 1.2 billion doses by the end of the year. This excess could have vaccinated every adult in sub-Saharan Africa with two doses.

Similar local disparities also occurred. The death rate in the lowest-income areas of the United States was nearly four and a half times higher than that in the wealthiest regions during the winter of 2020. Economically disadvantaged people face a greater risk of encountering infectious diseases due to their inability to work remotely, their reliance on public transportation, and the fact that they're more likely to live in densely populated areas with multiple family generations. And they are more likely to have underlying health conditions such as diabetes, asthma, or chronic pulmonary diseases, which increase their chances of severe illness if they contract an infectious disease.

As we look back on the lessons of the past, clearly, science and technology have equipped us with powerful tools to combat infectious diseases and protect public health. Our ability to respond to future pandemics will depend not only on our scientific advancements but also on our capacity to address the social, political, and economic challenges that persist. Misinformation, public mistrust, and inequality remain significant barriers to effective disease prevention and control. We must learn from the experiences of COVID-19 and other pandemics to build a more resilient global health system—one that balances individual freedoms with collective responsibility, promotes equitable access to health care, and prioritizes truth over fear. It is essential to realize that infectious diseases have no borders. The degree to which other people and countries are at risk determines the risk to all of us. No one is safe until everyone is safe.

TIMELINE

ca. 400 CE	Early dengue symptoms in China
541	Plague of Justinian begins
1338–1339	Black Death origin traced to Kyrgyzstan
1346–1353	Black Death kills up to two hundred million people
1360–1363	Plague returns to London
1492–1600	Columbian Exchange diseases decimate Native populations
1666	End of second plague pandemic
1746	First English use of the term *malaria*
1780	Dengue outbreak in Philadelphia, Pennsylvania
1820	Quinine isolated from cinchona bark
1855	Start of third plague pandemic in China
1894	*Yersinia pestis* discovered in Hong Kong
1898	Fleas confirmed as plague vectors
1901	Yellow fever virus identified
1905–1906	Yellow fever eradicated from Panama Canal Zone
1918	Influenza pandemic begins
1922	Massive dengue outbreak in Southeastern United States
1931	Electron microscope invented
1943–1946	Aerial DDT spraying eliminates dengue in the United States
1960	WHO ends third plague pandemic
1967	Project 523 initiated for malaria treatment

1971	Artemisinin discovered
1972	DDT banned in the United States
1980	Smallpox eradicated
1996	H5N1 bird flu emerges in China
2002–2003	SARS outbreak (SARS-CoV-1)
2005	1918 flu virus genetically sequenced
2006	Deadly bird flu outbreak
2009	Swine flu (H1N1) pandemic
2012	MERS-CoV identified in Saudi Arabia
2016	Anthrax outbreak from thawed permafrost
2020	COVID-19 declared a pandemic
2021	Omicron variant emerges
2022	Mass US bird culling due to H5N1
2023	H5N1 in marine mammals
2024	Omicron remains dominant

GLOSSARY

ANTIGEN: a molecule that the immune system recognizes as foreign or abnormal. Antigens trigger an immune response in the body.

BACILLUS: a rod-shaped bacterium found commonly in soil and water

BACTERIA: microscopic, single-celled organisms that lack a distinct nucleus and membrane-bound organelles. They were among the first life-forms to appear on Earth, about four billion years ago. While some bacteria can cause disease, most are harmless or even beneficial, such as those in the human gut microbiome.

BLACK DEATH: a bubonic plague pandemic that occurred in Europe from 1346 to 1666. It was the second major plague pandemic in European history.

BUBO: a swollen, painful lymph node. Buboes are a characteristic symptom of bubonic plague.

CHOLERA: acute diarrheal infection caused by ingestion of food or water contaminated with the bacterium *Vibrio cholerae*. It primarily affects the intestines and can lead to severe dehydration, shock, and death if untreated.

CONTACT TRACING: a method used to identify and notify people who have been exposed to an infectious disease. It is a useful tool for controlling the spread of infectious diseases, as it allows public health officials to quickly identify and isolate new cases before they can infect more people.

DISINFORMATION: false information that is deliberately and covertly spread to influence public opinion or obscure the truth

ELECTRON MICROSCOPE: a type of microscope that uses a beam of accelerated electrons, not light, as an illumination source. Electron microscopes are used to obtain information about the structure, shape, and composition of objects so small they can't be seen under light microscopes.

ENDEMIC: a disease consistently present within a specific population or geographic area. They can be severe or mild, and they can transition to epidemic status if their numbers significantly increase above the average number of cases.

EPIDEMIC: a disease outbreak characterized by a significantly greater number of disease cases than what is normally expected in that population

EXCESS MORTALITY: the number of extra deaths that surpasses the number that would have been expected under normal conditions—that is, without a disease outbreak. It is a holistic view, encompassing both confirmed and unreported fatalities and deaths from various causes that can be attributed to the disease.

FECAL-ORAL TRANSMISSION: when infectious agents found in the feces (stool) of an infected animal or person are ingested by another animal, leading to the spread of disease

GASTROENTERITIS: often referred to as stomach flu, an inflammation of the lining of the stomach and intestines, typically resulting in symptoms such as diarrhea, vomiting, abdominal pain or cramps, nausea, and sometimes fever

GENE: a sequence of nucleotides in DNA or RNA, passed from parents to offspring, encoding for proteins, or functional RNA molecules. Genes are the fundamental units of inheritance.

GENE REASSORTMENT: what occurs in segmented RNA viruses, such as the influenza virus, where coinfection of a host cell with multiple viruses can result in the shuffling of gene segments between viruses to generate new viruses with novel gene combinations

GENOME: the complete set of DNA or RNA instructions in a cell. It contains all the information necessary for an individual's development and function. It is the hereditary blueprint for life encoded in the DNA or RNA nucleotide sequence.

GERM THEORY: a theory stating that microscopic organisms, known as pathogens, or germs, can cause diseases by invading humans, animals, and other living hosts. These pathogens include bacteria, viruses, fungi, protists, and prions.

GLYCOPROTEINS: a protein that has a carbohydrate (sugar) molecule bound to it. Glycoproteins have diverse functions in cell surface receptors and can recognize and adhere to other cells.

HEMAGGLUTININ (H): a glycoprotein found on the surface of influenza viruses that is responsible for binding the virus to host cells and facilitating viral entry

HEMORRHAGING: the medical term for excessive or uncontrolled bleeding from a damaged blood vessel

IMMUNE SYSTEM: a complex network of organs, cells, and proteins that work together to recognize and eliminate harmful substances, promote healing, and defend the body against infections and diseases

INFECTION: when pathogens enter a person's body and multiply, leading to illness, organ and tissue damage, or disease

INFECTIOUS DISEASE: an illness resulting from pathogens that enter the body that can spread from person to person through contaminated food or water, contact with an infected person or animal, and bug bites

INFODEMIC: an overabundance of information, including false or misleading information, that makes it challenging for individuals to find trustworthy sources and reliable guidance during a disease outbreak

LIGHT MICROSCOPE: a type of microscope that uses visible light and a system of lenses to generate magnified images of small objects. The maximum practical magnification is typically about one thousand times. Electron microscopes are used for higher magnifications.

LIPID NANOPARTICLE: a spherical sac composed of lipids that serves as a novel drug delivery system in pharmaceuticals and biotechnology

LYMPHATIC SYSTEM: an essential part of the immune system in vertebrates, comprising a network of lymphatic vessels, lymph nodes, lymphoid organs, and lymphatic tissue. It carries lymph, a clear fluid, back to the heart for recirculation. Among many other processes, it is responsible for facilitating immune responses by transporting antigen-presenting cells to lymph nodes.

MIASMA THEORY: an outdated theory that diseases come from inhaling poisonous or bad air called miasma

MISINFORMATION: false information that is accidentally generated and spread

MODEL ORGANISM: an organism, such as a fruit fly or a mouse, that is extensively studied to understand biological phenomena, such as human diseases, when human experimentation is unethical or unfeasible

MUTATION: a permanent alteration that occurs in an organism's DNA or RNA sequence. Mutations can improve a pathogen's virulence and ability to evade host immune systems and drug therapies.

NEURAMINIDASE: an enzyme found on the surface of influenza viruses that plays a crucial role in viral infection and replication. It enables the influenza virus to be released from the host cell after replication.

PANDEMIC: the worldwide spread of a new or mutated disease that affects many people across multiple countries and continents

PATHOGEN: an organism that can cause disease in its host. They include viruses, bacteria, fungi, protozoa, and some multicellular organisms such as parasitic worms.

PATHOGENESIS: how a disease or disorder develops. It includes the factors contributing to a disease's onset, progression, and continuation.

RECOMBINATION: how genetic material is exchanged between different organisms, producing offspring with combinations of traits that differ from those found in either parent

REPRODUCTIVE NUMBER: represented as R_0 (pronounced "R-naught" or "R-zero"), a key epidemiological metric that represents the average number of new infections caused by a single infected individual in a completely susceptible population (one that is not vaccinated, masking, or taking other preventive measures)

RESERVOIR: of a disease, the habitat—either the population of organisms or the specific environment—where a pathogen normally resides

SEPTICEMIA: also known as blood poisoning, a serious and potentially life-threatening bloodstream infection that occurs when bacteria (and sometimes their toxins) enter the bloodstream from another part of the body, such as the skin, lungs, urinary tract, or abdomen

SEQUENCING: determining the order of nucleotides in DNA or RNA molecules. It provides essential information for understanding the genetic makeup of organisms and pathogens, diagnosing genetic diseases, and developing treatments.

SEROTYPE: a distinct variation within a species of bacteria, virus, or other microorganism that is classified based on its surface antigens

SPILLOVER: the transmission of a pathogen from an animal to a human; also known as a zoonotic spillover or pathogen spillover

SUPER-SPREADER: an individual who is highly contagious and capable of transmitting an infectious disease to an unusually enormous number of uninfected individuals

VACCINE: a treatment that stimulates the immune system to recognize and destroy specific disease-causing agents, thereby preventing or reducing the impact of infectious diseases

VECTOR: an organism that transmits infectious agents, such as pathogens, from one host to another, facilitating the spread of diseases; also known as a disease vector

VIRULENT: a highly infectious, toxic, or damaging pathogen

VIRUS: a submicroscopic infectious agent that can only replicate inside the living cells of another organism

WHITE BLOOD CELL: a crucial immune system component responsible for protecting the body against infections and foreign invaders. Also known as leukocytes, white blood cells are produced in the bone marrow and found throughout the body, including in the blood and lymphatic system.

SOURCE NOTES

58 "world's deadliest animal": "Fighting the World's Deadliest Animal," Centers for Disease Control and Prevention, August 14, 2024, https://www.cdc.gov/global-health/impact/fighting-the-worlds-deadliest-animal.html.

90 "We're not just . . . solidarity, not stigma.": T. A. Ghebreyesus, Munich Security Conference, opening speech, World Health Organization, February 15, 2020.

96 "speaking on gut instinct": M. S. Saag, "Misguided Use of Hydroxychloroquine for COVID-19: The Infusion of Politics into Science," *JAMA* 324, no. 21 (2020): 2161–2162.

98 "unreliable": "Journalism, Press Freedom and COVID," issue brief, UNESCO, 2020, https://unesdoc.unesco.org/ark:/48223/pf0000373573.

SELECTED BIBLIOGRAPHY

Barry, John M. *The Great Influenza: The Epic Story of the Deadliest Plague in History.* Penguin Books, 2005.

Goldin, Ian, and Mike Mariathasan. *The Butterfly Defect: How Globalization Creates Systemic Risks, and What to Do About It.* Princeton University Press, 2015.

Kelly, John. *The Great Mortality: An Intimate History of the Black Death, the Most Devastating Plague of All Time.* HarperCollins, 2005.

"Malaria Life Cycle Animation: Human Host—HHMI BioInteractive Video." Posted by biointeractive, June 12, 2014. YouTube video, 4:17. https://www.youtube.com/watch?v=Xaxjg9JOxug.

"Malaria Life Cycle Animation: Mosquito Host—HHMI BioInteractive Video." Posted by biointeractive, June 11, 2014. YouTube video, 3:59. https://www.youtube.com/watch?v=0uyE046It3o.

Offit, Paul A. *Tell Me When It's Over: An Expert's Guide to Deciphering COVID Myths and Navigating Our Post-Pandemic World.* National Geographic Partners, 2024.

Quammen, David. *Breathless: The Scientific Race to Defeat a Deadly Virus.* Simon & Schuster, 2022.

Quammen, David. *Spillover: Animal Infections and the Next Human Pandemic.* W. W. Norton, 2012.

Shah, Sonia. *The Fever: How Malaria Has Ruled Humankind for 500,000 Years.* Farrar, Straus and Giroux, 2010.

Tassier, Troy. *The Rich Flee and the Poor Take the Bus: How Our Unequal Society Fails Us During Outbreaks.* Johns Hopkins University Press, 2024.

Zimmer, Marc. *Illuminating Disease: An Introduction to Green Fluorescent Proteins.* Oxford University Press, 2015.

FURTHER INFORMATION

BOOKS

Kennedy, Jonathan. *Pathogenesis: A History of the World in Eight Plagues.* Crown, 2023.

Zimmer, Marc. *Science and the Skeptic: Discerning Fact from Fiction.* Twenty-First Century Books, 2022.

Zimmer, Marc. *Solutions for a Cleaner, Greener Planet: Environmental Chemistry.* Twenty-First Century Books, 2019.

WEBSITES

FluView
https://www.cdc.gov/fluview/index.html
FluView is the CDC's interactive web-based influenza surveillance report that provides weekly influenza activity estimates and other key flu surveillance data in the United States.

Nextstrain
https://nextstrain.org/
Nextstrain provides powerful analytics and interactive visualizations to aid epidemiological understanding, improve outbreak response, and provide real-time snapshots of evolving pathogen populations.

Our World in Data
https://ourworldindata.org/
Our World in Data uses interactive charts and maps to illustrate research findings that focus on large global problems such as poverty, disease, hunger, climate change, war, existential risks, and inequality.

INDEX

ABOUT THE AUTHOR

Marc Zimmer is the author of several nonfiction young adult books and a professor at Connecticut College, where he teaches chemistry and studies the proteins involved in producing light in jellyfish and fireflies. He received his PhD in chemistry from Worcester Polytechnic Institute and did his postdoc at Yale University. He has published articles on science and medicine for the *Los Angeles Times*, *USA Today*, and the *Huffington Post*, among many other publications. He lives in Waterford, Connecticut, with his wife.

PHOTO ACKNOWLEDGMENTS

Image credits: Designua/Shutterstock, p. 6; SANDIP NEOGI/Shutterstock, p. 8; Natalllenka.m/Shutterstock, p. 8 (mouse); Smith Collection/Gado/Getty Images, p. 9; Charles Phelps Cushing/ClassicStock/Getty Images, p. 11; Saloni Dattani (CC BY 4.0), p. 13; Zaporizhzhia vector/Shutterstock, p. 19; Alila Medical Media/Shutterstock, p. 27; Courtesy of Africa Center for Strategic Studies, p. 33; Edward "Doc" Rogers/MediaNews Group/Oakland Tribune/Getty Images, p. 35; Edwin Remsberg/Getty Images, p. 37; OurWorldinData.org/population-growth/CC BY 4.0, p. 42; Joao Paulo Burini/Getty Images, p. 44; Heritage Art/Heritage Images/Getty Images, p. 49; NOAA, 2024, p. 54; CA Dept of Public Health, p. 56; CDDEP, p. 62; Universal Images Group/Getty Images, p. 68; 2630ben/Getty Images, p. 73; Corona Borealis Studio/Shutterstock, p. 74; bojanstory/Getty Images, p. 80; CDC COVID Data Tracker, p. 86; Will Oliver/EPA/Bloomberg/Getty Images, p. 97; OurWorldinData.org/CC BY 4.0, p. 105.
Cover: kampee patisena/Getty Images.